To: _____

From: _____

Resources by Lee Strobel

The Case for Christ
The Case for Christ audio
The Case for Christ—Student Edition
  (with Jane Vogel)
The Case for a Creator
The Case for a Creator audio
The Case for a Creator—Student Edition
  (with Jane Vogel)
The Case for Easter
The Case for Faith
The Case for Faith audio
The Case for Faith—Student Edition
  (with Jane Vogel)
The Case for Faith Visual Edition
Experiencing the Passion of Jesus (with Garry Poole)
God's Outrageous Claims
Inside the Mind of Unchurched Harry and Mary
Surviving a Spiritual Mismatch in Marriage
  (with Leslie Strobel)
Surviving a Spiritual Mismatch in Marriage audio
What Jesus Would Say

THE CASE FOR CHRISTMAS

*A Journalist Investigates the Identity
of the Child in the Manger*

LEE STROBEL

GRAND RAPIDS, MICHIGAN 49530 USA

We want to hear from you. Please send your comments about this book to us in care of zreview@zondervan.com. Thank you.

ZONDERVAN™

The Case for Christmas
Copyright © 1998, 2005 by Lee Strobel

This book is excerpted from *The Case for Christ* by Lee Strobel, copyright © 1998 by Lee Strobel.

Requests for information should be addressed to:

Zondervan, *Grand Rapids, Michigan 49530*

ISBN-10: 0-310-25476-0
ISBN-13: 978-0-310-25476-8

Interior design by Michelle Espinoza

Edited by Rebecca Shingledecker

Printed in the United States of America

06 07 08 09 10 11 12 /❖ OPM/ 10 9 8 7 6

CONTENTS

INTRODUCTION:
WHO WAS IN THE MANGER ON THAT FIRST CHRISTMAS MORNING?

The *Chicago Tribune* newsroom was eerily quiet on the day before Christmas. As I sat at my desk with little to do, my mind kept wandering back to a family I had encountered a month earlier while I was working on a series of articles about Chicago's neediest people.

The Delgados—sixty-year-old Perfecta and her granddaughters Lydia and Jenny—had been burned out of their roach-infested tenement and were now living in a tiny two-room apartment on the West Side. As I walked in, I couldn't believe how empty it was. There was no furniture, no rugs, nothing on the walls—only a small kitchen table and one handful of rice. That's it. They were virtually devoid of possessions.

In fact, eleven-year-old Lydia and thirteen-year-old Jenny owned only one short-sleeved dress each, plus one thin, gray sweater between them. When they walked the half mile to school through the biting cold, Lydia would wear the sweater for part of the distance and then hand it to her shivering sister, who would wear it the rest of the way.

But despite their poverty and the painful arthritis that kept Perfecta from working, she still talked confidently about her faith in Jesus. She was convinced he had not abandoned them. I never sensed despair or self-pity in her home; instead, there was a gentle feeling of hope and peace.

7

I wrote an article about the Delgados and then quickly moved on to more exciting assignments. But as I sat at my desk on Christmas Eve, I continued to wrestle with the irony of the situation: here was a family that had nothing but faith and yet seemed happy, while I had everything I needed materially but lacked faith—and inside I felt as empty and barren as their apartment.

I walked over to the city desk to sign out a car. It was a slow news day with nothing of consequence going on. My boss could call me if something were to happen. In the meantime, I decided to drive over to West Homer Street and see how the Delgados were doing.

WHAT JESUS WOULD DO

When Jenny opened the door, I couldn't believe my eyes. *Tribune* readers had responded to my article by showering the Delgados with a treasure trove of gifts—roomfuls of furniture, appliances, and rugs; a lavish Christmas tree with piles of wrapped presents underneath; carton upon bulging carton of food; and a dazzling selection of clothing, including dozens of warm winter coats, scarves, and gloves. On top of that, they donated thousands of dollars in cash.

But as surprised as I was by this outpouring, I was even more astonished by what my visit was interrupting: Perfecta and her granddaughters were getting ready to give away much of their newfound wealth. When I asked Perfecta why, she replied in halting English: "Our neighbors are still in need. We cannot have plenty while they have nothing. This is what Jesus would want us to do."

That blew me away! If I had been in their position at that time in my life, I would have been hoarding everything. I asked Perfecta what she thought about the generosity of the people who had sent all of these goodies, and again her response amazed me.

"This is wonderful; this is very good," she said, gesturing toward the largess. "We did nothing to deserve this—it's a gift from God. But," she added, "it is not his greatest gift. No, we celebrate that tomorrow. That is Jesus."

To her, this child in the manger was the undeserved gift that meant everything—more than material possessions, more than comfort, more than security. And at that moment, something inside of me wanted desperately to know this Jesus—because, in a sense, I saw him in Perfecta and her granddaughters.

They had peace despite poverty, while I had anxiety despite plenty; they knew the joy of generosity, while I only knew the loneliness of ambition; they looked heavenward for hope, while I only looked out for myself; they experienced the wonder of the spiritual while I was shackled to the shallowness of the material—and something made me long for what they had.

Or, more accurately, for the One they knew.

I was pondering this as I drove back toward Tribune Tower a short time later. Suddenly, though, my thoughts were interrupted by the crackle of the car's two-way radio. It was my boss, sending me out on another assignment. Jarred back to reality, I let the emotions I felt in the Delgado apartment dissipate. And that, I figured at the time, was probably a good thing.

As I would caution myself whenever the Delgados would come to mind from time to time over the ensuing years, I'm not the sort of person who's driven by feelings. As a journalist, I was far more interested in facts, evidence, data, and concrete reality. Virgins don't get pregnant, there is no God who became a baby, and Christmas is little more than an annual orgy of consumption driven by the greed of corporate America.

Or so I thought.

EMBARKING ON AN INVESTIGATION

As a youngster, like countless other wide-eyed children, I listened with rapt fascination to the annual Bible story about Christmas. But as I matured, skepticism set in. I concluded that not only is Santa Claus merely a feel-good fable, but that the entire Christmas tale was itself built on a flimsy foundation of wishful thinking.

Sure, believing in Jesus could provide solace to sincere but simple folks like the Delgados; yes, it could spark feelings of hope and faith for people who prefer fantasy over reality. But as a law-trained newspaperman, I dealt in the currency of facts—and I was convinced they supported my atheism rather than Christianity.

All of that changed several years later, however, when I took a cue from one of the most famous Bible passages about Christmas. The story describes how an angel announced to a ragtag group of sheepherders that "a Savior who is Messiah and Master" had been born in David's town. Was this a hoax? A hallucination? Or could it actually be the pivotal event of human history—the incarnation of the living God?

The sheepherders were determined to get to the bottom of the matter. Like first-century investigative reporters being dispatched to the scene of an earth-shattering story, they declared: "Let's get over to Bethlehem as fast as we can and see for ourselves what God has revealed to us." They left, running, to check out the evidence for themselves.[1]

Essentially, that's what I did for a living as a *Tribune* reporter: investigate claims to see if they're true, separate rumors from reality, and determine facts from fiction. So prompted by my agnostic wife's conversion to Christianity, and still intrigued by memories of the Delgados, I decided to get to the bottom of what I now consider to be the most crucial issue of history: *Who was in the manger on that first Christmas morning?*

Even after two millennia, controversy continues to swirl around that issue. "Scholarly debate is intensifying over who Jesus actually was: divine, human, or both?" said a recent *Tribune* article. "Jesus has been portrayed in a burst of books as, among other things, a cynic philosopher, an apocalyptic prophet, a zealot, a rabbi, a Pharisee, a feminist, a radical egalitarian, and a postmodern social critic."

The Case for Christmas seeks to get to the bottom of this matter by retracing and expanding upon my original investigation into the roots of this cherished holiday. Can we really trust the biographies of Jesus to tell us the true story of his birth, life, teachings, miracles, death, and ultimate resurrection from the dead? Did the Christmas child actually grow up to fulfill the attributes of God? And did the baby in Bethlehem miraculously match the prophetic "fingerprint" of the long-awaited Messiah?

Join me in separating hard evidence from holiday tradition and sentiment. One thing is clear: as it was for me, this quest could very well become the most important endeavor of your life.

1

THE EYEWITNESS EVIDENCE: CAN THE BIOGRAPHIES OF JESUS BE TRUSTED?

When I first met soft-spoken Leo Carter, he was a seventeen-year-old veteran of Chicago's grittiest neighborhood. His testimony had put three killers in prison. And he was still carrying a .38-caliber slug in his head—a grisly reminder of a horrific saga that began when he witnessed Elijah Baptist gun down a local grocer.

Leo and a friend, Leslie Scott, were playing basketball when they saw Elijah, then sixteen years old, slay Sam Blue outside his grocery store. Leo had known the grocer since childhood. "When we didn't have any food, he'd give us some," Leo explained to me. "So when I went to the hospital and they said he was dead, I knew I'd have to testify about what I saw."

Eyewitness testimony is powerful. One of the most dramatic moments in a trial is when a witness describes the crime that he or she saw and then points confidently toward the defendant as being the perpetrator. Elijah Baptist knew that the only way to avoid prison would be to somehow prevent Leo Carter and Leslie Scott from doing just that.

So Elijah and two of his pals staged an ambush. Leslie and Leo's brother, Henry, were brutally murdered, while Leo was shot in the head and left for dead. But somehow, against all odds, Leo lived. The bullet, in a place too precarious to be removed, remained in his skull. Despite searing headaches that strong medication couldn't dull, he became the sole eye-witness against Elijah Baptist and his two cohorts. His word was good enough to land them in prison for the rest of their lives.

Leo Carter is one of my heroes. He made sure justice was served, even though he paid a monumental price for it. When I think of eyewitness testimony, even to this day—thirty years later—his face still appears in my mind.[2]

TESTIMONY FROM DISTANT TIME

Yes, eyewitness testimony can be compelling and con-vincing. When a witness has had ample opportunity to observe a crime, when there's no bias or ulterior motives, when the witness is truthful and fair, the climactic act of pointing out a defendant in a courtroom can be enough to doom that person to prison or worse.

And eyewitness testimony is just as crucial in investi-gating historical matters—even the issue of whether the Christmas manger really contained the unique Son of God.

But what eyewitness accounts do we possess? Do we have the testimony of anyone who personally interacted with Jesus, who listened to his teachings, who saw his mir-acles, who witnessed his death, and who encountered him after his alleged resurrection? Do we have any records from first-century "journalists" who interviewed eyewitnesses, asked tough questions, and faithfully recorded what they scrupulously determined to be true?

I knew that just as Leo Carter's testimony clinched the convictions of three brutal murderers, eyewitness accounts from the mists of distant time could help resolve the most important spiritual issue of all. To get solid answers, I flew to Denver to interview a scholar who literally wrote the book on the topic: Dr. Craig Blomberg, author of *The Historical Reliability of the Gospels.*

INTERVIEW: CRAIG L. BLOMBERG, PHD

Craig Blomberg is widely considered one of the country's foremost authorities on the biographies of Jesus, which are called the four gospels. He received his doctorate in New Testament from Aberdeen University in Scotland, later serving as a senior research fellow for Tyndale House at Cambridge University in England, where he was part of an elite group of international scholars that produced a series of acclaimed works on Jesus. He is currently a professor of New Testament at Denver Seminary.

As he settled into a high-back chair in his office, cup of coffee in hand, I too sipped some coffee to ward off the Colorado chill. Because I sensed Blomberg was a get-to-the-point kind of guy, I decided to start my interview by cutting to the core of the issue.

"Tell me this," I said with an edge of challenge in my voice, "is it really possible to be an intelligent, critically thinking person and still believe that the four gospels were written by the people whose names have been attached to them?"

Blomberg set his coffee cup on the edge of his desk and looked intently at me. "The answer is yes," he said with conviction.

He sat back and continued. "It's important to acknowledge that strictly speaking, the gospels are anonymous. But the uniform testimony of the early church was that Matthew, also known as Levi, the tax collector and one of the twelve disciples, was the author of the first gospel in the New Testament; that John Mark, a companion of Peter, was the author of the gospel we call Mark; and that Luke, known as Paul's 'beloved physician,' wrote both the gospel of Luke and the Acts of the Apostles."

"How uniform was the belief that they were the authors?" I asked.

"There are no known competitors for these three gospels," he said. "Apparently, it was just not in dispute."

Even so, I wanted to test the issue further. "Excuse my skepticism," I said, "but would anyone have had a motivation to lie by claiming these people wrote these gospels, when they really didn't?"

Blomberg shook his head. "Probably not. Remember, these were unlikely characters," he said, a grin breaking on his face. "Mark and Luke weren't even among the twelve disciples. Matthew was, but as a former hated tax collector, he would have been the most infamous character next to Judas Iscariot, who betrayed Jesus!

"Contrast this with what happened when the fanciful Apocryphal Gospels were written much later. People chose the names of well-known and exemplary figures to be their fictitious authors—Philip, Peter, Mary, James. Those names carried much more weight than the names of Matthew, Mark, and Luke. So to answer your question, there would not have been any reason to attribute authorship to these three less respected people if it weren't true."

That sounded logical, but it was obvious that he was leaving out one of the gospel writers. "What about John?" I asked. "He was extremely prominent; in fact, he wasn't just one of the twelve disciples but one of Jesus' inner three, along with James and Peter."

"Yes, he's the one exception," Blomberg conceded with a nod. "And interestingly, John is the only gospel about which there is some question of authorship."

"What exactly is in dispute?"

"The name of the author isn't in doubt—it's certainly John," Blomberg replied. "The question is whether it was John the apostle or a different John.

"You see, the testimony of a Christian writer named Papias, dated about AD 125, refers to John the apostle and John the elder, and it's not clear from the context whether he's talking about one person from two perspectives or two different people. But granted that exception, the rest of the early testimony is unanimous that it was John the apostle—the son of Zebedee—who wrote the gospel."

"And," I said in an effort to pin him down further, "you're convinced that he did?"

"Yes, I believe the substantial majority of the material goes back to the apostle," he replied. "However, if you read the gospel closely, you can see some indication that its concluding verses may have been finalized by an editor. Personally, I have no problem believing that somebody closely associated with John may have functioned in that role, putting the last verses into shape and potentially creating the stylistic uniformity of the entire document.

"But in any event," he stressed, "the gospel is obviously based on eyewitness material, as are the other three gospels."

DELVING INTO SPECIFICS

While I appreciated Blomberg's comments so far, I wasn't ready to move on yet. The issue of who wrote the Gospels is tremendously important, and I wanted specific details—names, dates, quotations. I finished off my coffee and put the cup on his desk. Pen poised, I prepared to dig deeper.

"Let's go back to Matthew, Mark, and Luke," I said. "What specific evidence do you have that they are the authors of the Gospels?"

Blomberg leaned forward. "Again, the oldest and probably most significant testimony comes from Papias, who in about AD 125 specifically affirmed that Mark had carefully and accurately recorded Peter's eyewitness observations. In fact, he said Mark 'made no mistake' and did not include 'any false statement.' And Papias said Matthew had preserved the teachings of Jesus as well.

"Then Irenaeus, writing about AD 180, confirmed the traditional authorship. In fact, here—," he said, reaching for a book. He flipped it open and read Irenaeus' words:

> Matthew published his own Gospel among the Hebrews in their own tongue, when Peter and Paul were preaching the Gospel in Rome and founding the church there. After their departure, Mark, the disciple and interpreter of Peter, himself handed down to us in writing the substance of Peter's preaching. Luke, the follower of Paul, set down in a book the Gospel preached by his teacher. Then John, the disciple of the Lord, who also leaned on his breast, himself produced his Gospel while he was living at Ephesus in Asia.[3]

I looked up from the notes I was taking. "Okay, let me clarify this," I said. "If we can have confidence that the gospels were written by the disciples Matthew and John; by

Mark, the companion of the disciple Peter; and by Luke, the historian, companion of Paul, and sort of a first-century journalist, we can be assured that the events they record are based on either direct or indirect eyewitness testimony."

As I was speaking, Blomberg was mentally sifting my words. When I finished, he nodded.

"Exactly," he said crisply.

ANCIENT VERSUS MODERN BIOGRAPHIES

There were still some troubling aspects of the gospels that I needed to resolve. In particular, I wanted to better understand the kind of literary genre they represented.

"When I go to the bookstore and look in the biography section, I don't see the same kind of writing that I see in the gospels," I said. "When somebody writes a biography these days, they thoroughly delve into the person's life. But look at Mark—he doesn't talk about the birth of Jesus or really anything through Jesus' early adult years. Instead he focuses on a three-year period and spends half his gospel on the events leading up to and culminating in Jesus' last week. How do you explain that?"

WHEN WAS JESUS BORN?

History doesn't pinpoint Jesus' birthday. Spring is most likely, because shepherds were watching their flocks at night and this is when ewes bore their young. In fact, around AD 200, theologians concluded Jesus was born on May 20. "Others," said journalist Terry Mattingly, "argued for dates in April and March. This wasn't a major issue, since early Christians emphasized the Epiphany on January 6, marking Christ's baptism."

In AD 385, Pope Julius I declared December 25 as the day for celebrating Christ's birth. "He chose that date," Christian researcher Gretchen Passantino told me, "partly to challenge the pagan celebration of the Roman god Saturnalia, which was characterized by social disorder and immorality."

Blomberg held up a couple of fingers. "There are two reasons," he replied. "One is literary and the other is theological.

"The literary reason is that basically, this is how people wrote biographies in the ancient world. They did not have the sense, as we do today, that it was important to give equal proportion to all periods of an individual's life or that it was necessary to tell the story in strictly chronological order or even to quote people verbatim, as long as the essence of what they said was preserved. Ancient Greek and Hebrew didn't even have a symbol for quotation marks.

"The only purpose for which they thought history was worth recording was because there were some lessons to be learned from the characters described. Therefore, the biographer wanted to dwell at length on those portions of the person's life that were exemplary, that were illustrative, that could help other people, that gave meaning to a period of history."

"And what's the theological reason?" I asked.

"It flows out of the point I just made. Christians believe that as wonderful as Jesus' life and teachings and miracles were, they were meaningless if it were not historically factual that Christ died and was raised from the dead and that this provided atonement, or forgiveness, of the sins of humanity.

"So Mark in particular, as the writer of probably the earliest gospel, devotes roughly half his narrative to the events leading up to and including one week's period of time and culminating in Christ's death and resurrection.

"Given the significance of the crucifixion," he concluded, "this makes perfect sense in ancient literature."

THE MYSTERY OF Q

In addition to the four gospels, scholars often refer to what they call *Q*, which stands for the German word *Quelle*, or "source." Because of similarities in language and content, it has traditionally been assumed that Matthew and Luke drew upon Mark's earlier gospel in writing their own. In addition, scholars have said that Matthew and Luke also incorporated some material from this mysterious *Q*, material that is absent from Mark.

"What exactly is *Q*?" I asked Blomberg.

"It's nothing more than a hypothesis," he replied, again leaning back comfortably in his chair. "With few exceptions, it's just sayings or teachings of Jesus, which once may have formed an independent, separate document.

"You see, it was a common literary genre to collect the sayings of respected teachers, sort of as we compile the top music of a singer and put it into a 'best of' album. *Q* may have been something like that. At least that's the theory."

But if *Q* existed before Matthew and Luke, it would constitute early material about Jesus. Perhaps, I thought, it can shed some fresh light on what Jesus was really like.

"Let me ask this," I said. "If you isolate just the material from Q, what kind of picture of Jesus do you get?"

Blomberg stroked his beard and stared at the ceiling for a moment as he pondered the question. "Well, you have to keep in mind that Q was a collection of sayings, and therefore it didn't have the narrative material that would have given us a more fully orbed picture of Jesus," he replied, speaking slowly as he chose each word with care.

"Even so, you find Jesus making some very strong claims—for instance, that he was wisdom personified and that he was the one by whom God will judge all humanity, whether they confess him or disavow him. A significant scholarly book has argued recently that if you isolate all the Q sayings, one actually gets the same kind of picture of Jesus—of someone who made audacious claims about himself—as you find in the gospels more generally."

I wanted to push him further on this point. "Would he be seen as a miracle worker?" I inquired.

"Again," he replied, "you have to remember that you wouldn't get many miracle stories per se, because they're normally found in the narrative, and Q is primarily a list of sayings."

He stopped to reach over to his desk, pick up a leather-bound Bible, and rustle through its well-worn pages.

"But, for example, Luke 7:18–23 and Matthew 11:2–6 say that John the Baptist sent his messengers to ask Jesus if he really was the Christ, the Messiah they were waiting for. Jesus replied in essence, 'Tell him to consider my miracles. Tell him what you've seen: the blind see, the deaf hear, the lame walk, the poor have good news preached to them.'

"So even in *Q*," he concluded, "there is clearly an aware-ness of Jesus' ministry of miracles."

Blomberg's mention of Matthew brought to mind another question concerning how the gospels were put together. "Why," I asked, "would Matthew—purported to be an eyewitness to Jesus—incorporate part of a gospel written by Mark, who everybody agrees was not an eye-witness? If Matthew's gospel was really written by an eye-witness, you would think he would have relied on his own observations."

Blomberg smiled. "It only makes sense if Mark was indeed basing his account on the recollections of the eye-witness Peter," he said. "As you've said yourself, Peter was among the inner circle of Jesus and was privy to seeing and hearing things that other disciples didn't. So it would make sense for Matthew, even though he was an eyewit-ness, to rely on Peter's version of events as transmitted through Mark."

THE UNIQUE PERSPECTIVE OF JOHN

Feeling satisfied with Blomberg's initial answers con-cerning the first three gospels—called the Synoptics, which means "to view at the same time," because of their similar outline and interrelationship—next I turned my atten-tion to John's gospel. Anyone who reads all four gospels will immediately recognize that there are obvious differences between the Synoptics and the gospel of John, and I wanted to know whether this means there are irreconcilable con-tradictions between them.

"Could you clarify the differences between the Syn-optic Gospels and John's gospel?" I asked Blomberg.

His eyebrows shot up. "*Huge* question!" he exclaimed.

After I assured him I was only after the essentials of the issue, not an exhaustive discussion, he settled back into his chair.

"Well, it's true that John is more different than similar to the Synoptics," he began. "Only a handful of the major stories that appear in the other three gospels reappear in John, although that changes noticeably when one comes to Jesus' last week. From that point forward the parallels are much closer.

"There also seems to be a very different linguistic style. In John, Jesus uses different terminology, he speaks in long sermons, and there seems to be a higher Christology— that is, more direct and more blatant claims that Jesus is one with the Father; God himself; the way, the truth, and the life; the resurrection and the life."

"What accounts for the differences?" I asked.

"For many years the assumption was that John knew everything Matthew, Mark, and Luke wrote, and he saw no need to repeat it, so he consciously chose to supplement them. More recently it has been assumed that John is largely independent of the other three gospels, which could account for not only the different choices of material, but also the different perspectives on Jesus."

JESUS' MOST AUDACIOUS CLAIM

"There are some theological distinctions to John," I observed.

"No question, but do they deserve to be called contradictions? I think the answer is no, and here's why: for almost every major theme or distinctive in John, you can find parallels in Matthew, Mark, and Luke, even if they're not as plentiful."

That was a bold assertion. I promptly decided to put it to the test by raising perhaps the most significant issue of all concerning the differences between the Synoptics and John's gospel.

"John makes very explicit claims of Jesus being God, which some attribute to the fact that he wrote later than the others and began embellishing things," I said. "Can you find this theme of deity in the Synoptics?"

"Yes, I can," he said. "It's more implicit but you find it there. Think of the story of Jesus walking on the water, found in Matthew 14:22–33 and Mark 6:45–52. Most English translations hide the Greek by quoting Jesus as saying, 'Fear not, it is I.' Actually, the Greek literally says, 'Fear not, I am.' Those last two words are identical to what Jesus said in John 8:58, when he took upon himself the divine name 'I am,' which is the way God revealed himself to Moses in the burning bush in Exodus 3:14. So Jesus is revealing himself as the one who has the same divine power over nature as Yahweh, the God of the Old Testament."

I nodded. "That's one example," I said. "Do you have any others?"

"Yes, I could go on along these lines," Blomberg said. "For instance, Jesus' most common title for himself in the first three gospels is 'Son of Man,' and—"

I raised my hand to stop him. "Hold on," I said. Reaching into my briefcase, I pulled out a book and leafed through it until I located the quote I was looking for. "Karen Armstrong, the former nun who wrote the bestseller *A History of God*, said it seems that the term 'Son of Man' 'simply stressed the weakness and mortality of the human condition,' so by using it, Jesus was merely emphasizing that 'he was a frail human being who would one day suffer and die.'[4] If that's true," I said, "that doesn't sound like much of a claim to deity."

Blomberg's expression turned sour. "Look," he said firmly, "contrary to popular belief, 'Son of Man' does not primarily refer to Jesus' humanity. Instead it's a direct allusion to Daniel 7:13–14."

With that he opened the Old Testament and read those words of the prophet Daniel.

> In my vision at night I looked, and there before me was one like a son of man, coming with the clouds of heaven. He approached the Ancient of Days and was led into his presence. He was given authority, glory and sovereign power; all peoples, nations and men of every language worshiped him. His dominion is an everlasting dominion that will not pass away, and his kingdom is one that will never be destroyed.

Blomberg shut the Bible. "So look at what Jesus is doing by applying the term 'Son of Man' to himself," he continued. "This is someone who approaches God himself in his heavenly throne room and is given universal authority and dominion. That makes 'Son of Man' a title of great exaltation, not of mere humanity."

Later I came upon a comment by another scholar, Dr. William Lane Craig, who has made a similar observation:

> "Son of Man" is often thought to indicate the humanity of Jesus, just as the reflex expression "Son

of God" indicates his divinity. In fact, just the opposite is true. The Son of Man was a divine figure in the Old Testament book of Daniel who would come at the end of the world to judge mankind and rule forever. Thus, the claim to be the Son of Man would be in effect a claim to divinity.[5]

Continued Blomberg: "In addition, Jesus claims to forgive sins in the Synoptics, and that's something only God can do. Jesus accepts prayer and worship. Jesus says, 'Whoever acknowledges me, I will acknowledge before my Father in heaven.' Final judgment is based on one's reaction to—whom? This mere human being? No, that would be a very arrogant claim. Final judgment is based on one's reaction to Jesus *as God*.

"As you can see, there's all sorts of material in the Synoptics about the deity of Christ, that then merely becomes more explicit in John's gospel."

THE GOSPELS' THEOLOGICAL AGENDA

In authoring the last gospel, John did have the advantage of being able to mull over theological issues for a longer period of time. So I asked Blomberg, "Doesn't the fact that John was writing with more of a theological bent mean that his historical material may have been tainted and therefore less reliable?"

"I don't believe John is more theological," Blomberg stressed. "He just has a different cluster of theological emphases. Matthew, Mark, and Luke each have very distinctive theological angles that they want to highlight: Luke, the theologian of the poor and of social concern; Matthew, the theologian trying to understand the relationship of

Christianity and Judaism; Mark, who shows Jesus as the suffering servant. You can make a long list of the distinctive theologies of Matthew, Mark, and Luke."

I interrupted because I was afraid Blomberg was missing my broader point. "Okay, but don't those theological motivations cast doubt on their ability and willingness to accurately report what happened?" I asked. "Isn't it likely that their theological agenda would prompt them to color and twist the history they recorded?"

"It certainly means that as with any ideological document, we have to consider that as a possibility," he admitted. "There are people with axes to grind who distort history to serve their ideological ends, but unfortunately people have concluded that always happens, which is a mistake.

"In the ancient world the idea of writing dispassionate, objective history merely to chronicle events, with no ideological purpose, was unheard of. Nobody wrote history if there wasn't a reason to learn from it."

I smiled. "I suppose you could say that makes everything suspect," I suggested.

"Yes, at one level it does," he replied. "But if we can reconstruct reasonably accurate history from all kinds of other ancient sources, we ought to be able to do that from the gospels, even though they too are ideological."

Blomberg thought for a moment, searching his mind for an appropriate analogy to drive home his point. Finally he said, "Here's a modern parallel, from the experience of the Jewish community, that might clarify what I mean.

"Some people, usually for anti-Semitic purposes, deny or downplay the horrors of the Holocaust. But it has been the Jewish scholars who've created museums, written books, preserved artifacts, and documented eyewitness testimony concerning the Holocaust.

"Now, they have a very ideological purpose—namely, to ensure that such an atrocity never occurs again—but they have also been the most faithful and objective in their reporting of historical truth.

"Christianity was likewise based on certain historical claims that God uniquely entered into space and time in the person of Jesus of Nazareth, so the very ideology that Christians were trying to promote required as careful historical work as possible."

He let his analogy sink in. Turning to face me more directly, he asked, "Do you see my point?"

I nodded to indicate that I did.

HOT NEWS FROM HISTORY

It's one thing to say that the gospels are rooted in direct or indirect eyewitness testimony; it's another to claim that this information was reliably preserved until it was finally written down years later. This, I knew, was a major point of contention, and I wanted to challenge Blomberg with this issue as forthrightly as I could.

Again I picked up Armstrong's popular book *A History of God*. "Listen to something else she wrote," I said.

We know very little about Jesus. The first full-length account of his life was St. Mark's gospel, which was not written until about the year 70, some forty years after his death. By that time, historical facts had been overlaid with mythical elements which expressed the meaning Jesus had acquired for his followers. It is this meaning that St. Mark primarily conveys rather than a reliable straightforward portrayal.[6]

Tossing the book back into my open briefcase, I turned to Blomberg and continued. "Some scholars say the gospels were written so far after the events that legend developed and distorted what was finally written down, turning Jesus from merely a wise teacher into the mythological Son of God. Is that a reasonable hypothesis, or is there good evidence that the gospels were recorded earlier than that, before legend could totally corrupt what was ultimately recorded?"

BELIEVING THE VIRGIN BIRTH

Though 79 percent of Americans believe the virgin birth, it was a stumbling block for philosopher William Lane Craig when he was young. "I thought it was absurd," he said. "For the virgin birth to be true, a Y chromosome had to be created out of nothing in Mary's ovum, because Mary didn't possess the genetic material to produce a male child."

Still, he became a Christian. "You don't need to have all your questions answered to come to faith," he told me. "You just have to say, 'The weight of the evidence seems to show this is true, so even though I don't have answers to all my questions, I'm going to believe and hope for answers in the long run.'"

Craig, who became an expert on scientific evidence for a Creator, later resolved the issue. "If I really do believe in a God who created the universe," Craig said, smiling, "then for him to create a Y chromosome would be child's play!"

Blomberg's eyes narrowed, and his voice took on an adamant tone. "There are two separate issues here, and it's important to keep them separate," he said. "I do think there's good evidence for suggesting early dates for the writing of the gospels. But even if there wasn't, Armstrong's argument doesn't work anyway."

"Why not?" I asked.

"The standard scholarly dating, even in very liberal circles, is Mark in the 70s, Matthew and Luke in the 80s, John in the 90s. But listen: that's still within the lifetimes of various eyewitnesses of the life of Jesus, including hostile eyewitnesses who would have served as a corrective if false teachings about Jesus were going around. Consequently, these late dates for the gospels really aren't all that late. In fact, we can make a comparison that's very instructive.

"The two earliest biographies of Alexander the Great were written by Arrian and Plutarch more than four hundred years after Alexander's death in 323 BC, yet historians consider them to be generally trustworthy. Yes, legendary material about Alexander did develop over time, but it was only in the centuries after these two writers.

"In other words, the first five hundred years kept Alexander's story pretty much intact; legendary material began to emerge over the next five hundred years. So whether the gospels were written sixty years or thirty years after the life of Jesus, the amount of time is negligible by comparison. It's almost a nonissue."

I could see what Blomberg was saying. At the same time, I had some reservations about it. To me, it seemed obvious that the shorter the gap between an event and when it was recorded in writing, the less likely those writings would fall victim to legend or faulty memories.

"Let me concede your point for the moment, but let's get back to the dating of the gospels," I said. "You indicated that you believe they were written sooner than the dates you mentioned."

"Yes, sooner," he said. "And we can support that by looking at the book of Acts, which was written by Luke. Acts ends apparently unfinished—Paul is a central figure of the book, and he's under house arrest in Rome. With that the book abruptly halts. What happens to Paul? We don't find out from Acts, probably because the book was written before Paul was put to death."

Blomberg was getting more wound up as he went. "That means Acts cannot be dated any later than AD 62. Having established that, we can then move backward from there. Since Acts is the second of a two-part work, we know the first part—the gospel of Luke—must have been written earlier than that. And since Luke incorporates parts of the gospel of Mark, that means Mark is even earlier.

"If you allow maybe a year for each of those, you end up with Mark written no later than about AD 60, maybe even the late 50s. If Jesus was put to death in AD 30 or 33, we're talking about a maximum gap of thirty years or so."

He sat back in his chair with an air of triumph. "Historically speaking, especially compared with Alexander the Great," he said, "that's like a news flash!"

Indeed, that was impressive, closing the gap between the events of Jesus' life and the writing of the gospels to the point where it was negligible by historical standards.

However, I still wanted to push the issue. My goal was to turn the clock back as far as I could to get to the very earliest information about Jesus.

GOING BACK TO THE BEGINNING

I stood and strolled over to the bookcase. "Let's see if we can go back even further," I said, turning toward Blomberg. "How early can we date the fundamental beliefs in Jesus' atonement, his resurrection, and his unique association with God?"

"It's important to remember that the books of the New Testament are not in chronological order," he began. "The gospels were written after almost all the letters of Paul, whose writing ministry probably began in the late 40s. Most of his major letters appeared during the 50s. To find the earliest information, one goes to Paul's epistles and then asks, 'Are there signs that even earlier sources were used in writing them?'"

"And," I prompted, "what do we find?"

"We find that Paul incorporated some creeds, confessions of faith, or hymns from the earliest Christian church. These go way back to the dawning of the church soon after the resurrection.

"The most famous creeds include Philippians 2:6–11, which talks about Jesus being 'in very nature God,' and Colossians 1:15–20, which describes him as being 'the image of the invisible God,' who created all things and through whom all things are reconciled with God 'by making peace through his blood, shed on the cross.'

"Those are certainly significant in explaining what the earliest Christians were convinced about Jesus. But perhaps the most important creed in terms of the historical Jesus is 1 Corinthians 15, where Paul uses technical language to indicate he was passing along this oral tradition in relatively fixed form."

Blomberg located the passage in his Bible and read it to me.

> For what I received I passed on to you as of first importance: that Christ died for our sins according to the Scriptures, that he was buried, that he was raised on the third day according to the Scriptures, and that he appeared to Peter, and then to the Twelve. After that, he appeared to more than five hundred of the brothers at the same time, most of whom are still living, though some have fallen asleep. Then he appeared to James, then to all the apostles.[7]

"And here's the point," Blomberg said. "If the crucifixion was as early as AD 30, Paul's conversion was about AD 32. Immediately Paul was ushered into Damascus, where he met with a Christian named Ananias and some other disciples. His first meeting with the apostles in Jerusalem would have been about AD 35. At some point along there, Paul was given this creed, which had already been formulated and was being used in the early church.

"Now, here you have the key facts about Jesus' death for our sins, plus a detailed list of those to whom he appeared in resurrected form—all dating back to within two to five years of the events themselves!

"That's not later mythology from forty or more years down the road, as Armstrong suggested. A good case can be made for saying that Christian belief in the resurrection, though not yet written down, can be dated to within two years of that very event.

"This is enormously significant," he said, his voice rising a bit in emphasis. "Now you're not comparing thirty to sixty years with the five hundred years that's generally acceptable for other data—you're talking about two!"

I couldn't deny the importance of that evidence. It certainly seemed to take the wind out of the charge that the resurrection—which is cited by Christians as the crowning confirmation of Jesus' divinity—was merely a mythological concept that developed over long periods of time as legends corrupted the eyewitness accounts of Christ's life.

For me, this struck especially close to home—as a skeptic, that was one of my biggest objections to Christianity.

Later I clicked my briefcase closed and stood to thank Blomberg. Our interview, reported in more detail in my book *The Case for Christ*, heightened my confidence in the overall reliability of the gospel accounts, including the Christmas story. Still, there were some vexing puzzles related to Jesus' birth that only an archaeologist could answer—and that led me to the author of the book *Archaeology and the New Testament*.

2

THE SCIENTIFIC EVIDENCE: DOES ARCHAEOLOGY CONFIRM OR CONTRADICT JESUS' BIOGRAPHIES?

There was something surreal about my lunch with Dr. Jeffrey MacDonald. There he was, casually munching on a tuna fish sandwich and potato chips in a conference room of a North Carolina courthouse, making upbeat comments and generally enjoying himself. In a nearby room a dozen jurors were taking a break after hearing gruesome evidence that MacDonald had brutally murdered his wife and two young daughters.

As we were finishing our meal, I couldn't restrain myself from asking MacDonald the obvious questions. "How can you act as if nothing is wrong?" I said, my voice mixed with astonishment and indignation. "Aren't you the slightest bit concerned that those jurors are going to find you guilty?"

MacDonald casually waved his half-eaten sandwich in the general direction of the jury room. "Them?" he chortled. "They'll never convict me!"

Then, apparently realizing how cynical those words sounded, he quickly added, "I'm innocent, you know."

That was the last time I ever heard him laugh. Within days the former Green Beret and emergency room physician was found guilty of stabbing to death his wife, Colette, and his daughters, Kimberly, age five, and Kristen, age two.

He was promptly sentenced to life in prison and carted off in handcuffs.

MacDonald was cocky enough to think that his alibi would help him get away with murder. He had told investigators that he was asleep on the couch when drug-crazed hippies awakened him in the middle of the night. He said he fought them off, getting stabbed and knocked unconscious in the process. When he awakened, he found his family slaughtered.

Detectives were skeptical from the start. The living room showed few signs of a life-and-death struggle, and MacDonald's wounds were superficial. Skepticism alone, however, doesn't win convictions; that requires hard evidence. In MacDonald's case detectives relied on scientific proof to untangle his web of lies and convict him of the slayings.

There's a wide variety of scientific evidence that's commonly used in trials, ranging from DNA typing to forensic anthropology to toxicology. In MacDonald's case it was serology (blood evidence) and trace evidence that dispatched him to the penitentiary.

In an extraordinary—and for prosecutors, fortuitous—coincidence, each member of MacDonald's family had a different blood type. By analyzing where bloodstains were found, investigators were able to reconstruct the sequence of events that deadly evening—and it directly contradicted MacDonald's version of what happened.

Scientific study of tiny blue pajama threads, which were found scattered in various locations, also refuted his alibi. And microscopic analysis demonstrated that holes in his pajamas could not have been made, as he claimed, by an ice pick wielded by the home invaders. In short, it was FBI technicians in white lab coats who were really behind Mac-Donald's conviction.[8]

Scientific evidence can also make important contributions to the question of whether the New Testament accounts of Jesus are accurate. While serology and toxicology aren't able to shed any light on the issue, another category of scientific proof—the discipline of archaeology—has great bearing on the reliability of the gospels.

Hundreds of archaeological findings from the first century have been unearthed, and I was curious: did they undermine or undergird the eyewitness stories about Jesus? So I went on a quest for a recognized authority who has personally dug among the ruins of the Middle East, who has an encyclopedic knowledge of ancient findings, and who possesses enough scientific restraint to acknowledge the limits of archaeology while at the same time explaining how it can illuminate life in the first century.

INTERVIEW: JOHN MCRAY, PHD

When scholars and students study archaeology, many turn to John McRay's thorough and dispassionate 432-page textbook, *Archaeology and the New Testament*.

McRay studied at Hebrew University, the École Biblique et Archéologique Française in Jerusalem, Vanderbilt University Divinity School, and the University of Chicago, where he earned his doctorate in 1967. McRay was a professor of New Testament and archaeology at Wheaton College for more than fifteen years.

Seeking to test whether he would overstate the influence of archaeology, I decided to open our interview by asking him what it *can't* tell us about the reliability of the New Testament.

"Archaeology has made some important contributions," he began, speaking in a drawl he picked up as a child in southeastern Oklahoma, "but it certainly can't prove whether the New Testament is the word of God. If we dig in Israel and find ancient sites that are consistent with where the Bible said we'd find them, that shows that its history and geography are accurate. However, it doesn't confirm that what Jesus Christ said is right. Spiritual truths cannot be proved or disproved by archaeological discoveries."

As an analogy, he offered the story of Heinrich Schliemann, who searched for Troy in an effort to prove the historical accuracy of Homer's *Iliad*. "He did find Troy," McRay observed with a gentle smile, "but that didn't prove the *Iliad* was true. It was merely accurate in a particular geographical reference."

Once we had set some boundaries for what archaeology can't establish, I was anxious to begin exploring what it *can* tell us about the New Testament. I decided to launch into this topic by making an observation that grew out of my experience as an investigative journalist with a legal background.

DIGGING FOR THE TRUTH

In trying to determine if a witness is being truthful, journalists and lawyers will test all the elements of his or her testimony that can be tested. If this investigation reveals that the person was wrong in those details, this casts considerable doubt on the veracity of his or her entire story. However, if the minutiae check out, this is some indication—not conclusive proof but some evidence—that maybe the witness is being reliable in his or her overall account.

For instance, if a man were telling about a trip he took from St. Louis to Chicago, and he mentioned that he had stopped in Springfield, Illinois, to see the movie *The Passion of the Christ* at the Odeon Theater and that he had eaten a large Clark bar he bought at the concession counter, investigators could determine whether such a theater exists in Springfield as well as if it was showing this particular film and selling this specific brand and size of candy bar at the time he said he was there. If their findings contradict what the person claimed, this seriously tarnishes his trustworthiness. If the details check out, this doesn't prove that his entire story is true, but it does enhance his reputation for being accurate.

In a sense, this is what archaeology accomplishes. The premise is that if an ancient historian's incidental details check out to be accurate time after time, this increases our confidence in other material that the historian wrote but that cannot be as readily cross-checked.

So I asked McRay for his professional opinion. "Does archaeology affirm or undermine the New Testament when it checks out the details in those accounts?"

McRay was quick to answer. "Oh, there's no question that the credibility of the New Testament is enhanced," he said, "just as the credibility of any ancient document is enhanced when you excavate and find that the author was accurate in talking about a particular place or event."

As an example, he brought up his own digs in Caesarea on the coast of Israel, where he and others excavated the harbor of Herod the Great.

"For a long time people questioned the validity of a statement by Josephus, the first-century historian, that this harbor was as large as the one at Piraeus, which is a major harbor of Athens. People thought Josephus was wrong, because when you see the stones above the surface of the water in the contemporary harbor, it's not very big.

"But when we began to do underwater excavation, we found that the harbor extended far out into the water underground, that it had fallen down, and that its total dimensions were indeed comparable to the harbor at Piraeus. So it turns out Josephus was right after all. This was one more bit of evidence that Josephus knew what he was talking about."

So what about the New Testament writers? Did they really know what they were talking about? I wanted to put that issue to the test in my next line of questioning.

LUKE'S ACCURACY AS A HISTORIAN

The physician and historian Luke authored both the gospel bearing his name and the book of Acts, which together constitute about one-quarter of the entire New Testament. The gospels of Luke and Matthew are the only ones to provide details about the birth story of Jesus.

Luke is believed to have personally interviewed eyewitnesses who knew about everything from the birth to the death to the resurrection of Jesus. In fact, this companion of the apostle Paul said he "carefully investigated everything" so he could "write an orderly account" about "the certainty" of what occurred.[9] There was no doubt that he was claiming to be recording actual historical events.

DID CHRISTIANITY COPY EARLIER MYTHS?

Skeptics claim Christianity, including the virgin birth, is merely a repackaging of pagan "mystery religions." Not true, says apologist Alex McFarland. Contrary to mythology, "the New Testament deals with actual persons and historical events open to investigation," he said.

Researcher Gretchen Passantino agrees that Christ's birth is radically different from these mythological tales. "For example, instead of a virgin willingly conceiving by the invisible power of God, the myths gave us lurid tales of lusty gods having forced sex with women," she said. "Instead of the Incarnation, the myths gave us half-human, half-divine superheroes subject to the same weaknesses, sins, and frustrations as we are."

Albert Schweitzer said those who claim Christianity was derived from these myths "manufacture out of the various fragments of information a kind of universal mystery religion which never existed." And C. S. Lewis confirmed Christianity originated "in a circle where no trace of the nature religion was present."

But I wanted to know whether Luke got things right. "When archaeologists check out the details of what he wrote," I said, "do they find that he was careful or sloppy?"

"The general consensus of both liberal and conservative scholars is that Luke is very accurate as a historian," McRay replied. "He's erudite, he's eloquent, his Greek approaches classical quality, he writes as an educated man, and archaeological discoveries are showing over and over again that Luke is accurate in what he has to say."

In fact, he added, there have been several instances, similar to the story about the harbor, in which scholars initially thought Luke was wrong in a particular reference, only to have later discoveries confirm that he was correct in what he wrote.

For instance, in Luke 3:1 he refers to Lysanias being the tetrarch of Abilene in about AD 27. For years scholars pointed to this as evidence that Luke didn't know what he was talking about, since everybody knew that Lysanias was not a tetrarch but rather the ruler of Chalcis half a century earlier. If Luke can't get that basic fact right, they suggested, then nothing he has written can be trusted.

That's when archaeology stepped in. "An inscription was later found from the time of Tiberius, from AD 14 to 37, which names Lysanias as tetrarch in Abila near Damascus—just as Luke had written," McRay explained. "It turned out there had been two government officials named Lysanias! Once more Luke was shown to be exactly right."

Another example is Luke's reference in Acts 17:6 to "politarchs," which is translated as "city officials" by the New International Version, in the city of Thessalonica. "For a long time people thought Luke was mistaken, because no evidence of the term *politarchs* had been found in any ancient Roman documents," McRay said.

"However, an inscription on a first-century arch was later found that begins, 'In the time of the politarchs . . .' You can go to the British Museum and see it for yourself. And then, lo and behold, archaeologists have found more than thirty-five inscriptions that mention politarchs, several of these in Thessalonica from the same period Luke was referring to. Once again the critics were wrong and Luke was shown to be right."

One prominent archaeologist carefully examined Luke's references to thirty-two countries, fifty-four cities, and nine islands, finding not a single mistake.[10]

Here's the bottom line: "If Luke was so painstakingly accurate in his historical reporting," said one book on the topic, "on what logical basis may we assume he was credulous or inaccurate in his reporting of matters that were far more important, not only to him but to others as well?"[11]

Matters, for example, like the resurrection of Jesus, the most influential evidence of his deity, which Luke says was firmly established by "many convincing proofs."[12]

THE RELIABILITY OF JOHN

Archaeology may support the credibility of Luke, but he isn't the only author of the New Testament. I wondered what scientists would have to say about John, who begins his gospel by eloquently affirming the incarnation—that is, "the Word," or Jesus, "became flesh and made his dwelling among us" on the first Christmas.[13]

John's gospel was sometimes considered suspect because he talked about locations that couldn't be verified. Some scholars charged that since he failed to get these basic details straight, John must not have been close to the events of Jesus' life.

That conclusion, however, has been turned upside down in recent years. "There have been several discoveries that have shown John to be very accurate," McRay pointed out. "For example, John 5:1–15 records how Jesus healed an invalid by the Pool of Bethesda. John provides the detail that the pool had five porticoes. For a long time people cited this as an example of John being inaccurate, because no such place had been found.

"But more recently the Pool of Bethesda has been excavated—it lies maybe forty feet below ground—and sure enough, there were five porticoes, which means colonnaded porches or walkways, exactly as John had described. And you have other discoveries—the Pool of Siloam from John 9:7, Jacob's Well from John 4:12, the probable location of the Stone Pavement near the Jaffa Gate where Jesus appeared before Pilate in John 19:13, even Pilate's own identity—all of which have lent historical credibility to John's gospel."

"So this challenges the allegation that the gospel of John was written so long after Jesus that it can't possibly be accurate," I said.

"Most definitely," he replied.

I decided to ask McRay a broader question: had he ever encountered any archaeological finding that blatantly contravened a New Testament reference?

He shook his head. "Archaeology has not produced anything that is unequivocally a contradiction to the Bible," he replied with confidence. "On the contrary, as we've seen, there have been many opinions of skeptical scholars that have become codified into 'fact' over the years but that archaeology has shown to be wrong."

Even so, there were some matters I needed to resolve, especially about issues revolving around the birth of Jesus. I pulled out my notes and got ready to challenge McRay with three long-standing riddles about Christmas-related issues that I thought archaeology might have trouble explaining.

PUZZLE 1: THE CENSUS

Luke's narrative claims that Mary and Joseph were required by a census to return to Joseph's hometown of

Bethlehem. "Let me be blunt: this seems absurd," I said. "How could the government possibly force all its citizens to return to their birthplace? Is there any archaeological evidence whatsoever that this kind of census ever took place?"

McRay calmly pulled out a copy of his book. "Actually, the discovery of ancient census forms has shed quite a bit of light on this practice," he said as he leafed through the pages. Finding the reference he was searching for, he quoted from an official governmental order dated AD 104.

> Gaius Vibius Maximus, Prefect of Egypt [says]: Seeing that the time has come for the house to house census, it is necessary to compel all those who for any cause whatsoever are residing out of their provinces to *return to their own homes*, that they may both carry out the regular order of the census and may also attend diligently to the cultivation of their allotments.[14]

"As you can see," he said as he closed the book, "that practice is confirmed by this document, even though this particular manner of counting people might seem odd to you. And another papyrus, this one from AD 48, indicates that the entire family was involved in the census."

This, however, did not entirely dispose of the issue. Luke said the census that brought Joseph and Mary to Bethlehem was conducted when Quirinius was governing Syria and during the reign of Herod the Great.

"That poses a significant problem," I pointed out, "because Herod died in 4 BC, and Quirinius didn't begin ruling Syria until AD 6, conducting the census soon after that. There's a big gap there; how can you deal with such a major discrepancy in the dates?"

McRay knew I was raising an issue that archaeologists have wrestled with for years. He responded by saying, "An eminent archaeologist named Jerry Vardaman has done a great deal of work in this regard. He has found a coin with the name of Quirinius on it in very small writing, or what we call 'micrographic' letters. This places him as proconsul of Syria and Cilicia from 11 BC until after the death of Herod."

I was confused. "What does that mean?" I asked.

"It means that there were apparently two Quiriniuses," he replied. "It's not uncommon to have lots of people with the same Roman names, so there's no reason to doubt that there were two people by the name of Quirinius. The census would have taken place under the reign of the earlier Quirinius. Given the cycle of a census every fourteen years, that would work out quite well."

PUZZLE 2: EXISTENCE OF NAZARETH

Many Christians are unaware that skeptics have been asserting for a long time that Nazareth never existed during the time when the New Testament says Jesus spent his childhood there after his birth in Bethlehem.

Atheist Frank Zindler has noted that Nazareth is not mentioned in the Old Testament, by the apostle Paul, by the Talmud, or by the first-century historian Josephus. In fact, no ancient historians or geographers mention Nazareth before the beginning of the fourth century.[15]

This absence of evidence paints a suspicious picture. So I put the issue directly to McRay: "Is there any archaeological confirmation that Nazareth was in existence during the first century?"

This issue wasn't new to McRay. "Dr. James Strange of the University of South Florida is an expert on this area, and he describes Nazareth as being a very small place, about sixty acres, with a maximum population of about four hundred and eighty at the beginning of the first century," McRay replied.

"How does he know that?" I asked.

"Well, Strange notes that when Jerusalem fell in AD 70, priests were no longer needed in the temple because it had been destroyed, so they were sent out to various other locations, even up into Galilee. Archaeologists have found a list in Aramaic describing the twenty-four 'courses,' or families, of priests who were relocated, and one of them was registered as having been moved to Nazareth. That shows that this tiny village must have been there at the time."

In addition, he said there have been archaeological digs that have uncovered first-century tombs in the vicinity of Nazareth, which would establish the village's limits, because by Jewish law, burials had to take place outside the town proper.

McRay picked up a copy of a book by renowned archaeologist Jack Finegan, published by Princeton University Press. He leafed through it, then read Finegan's analysis: "From the tombs . . . it can be concluded that Nazareth was a strongly Jewish settlement in the Roman period."[16]

McRay looked up at me. "There has been discussion about the location of some sites from the first century, such as exactly where Jesus' tomb is situated, but among archaeologists there has never really been a big doubt about the location of Nazareth. The burden of proof ought to be on those who dispute its existence."

That seemed reasonable. Even the usually skeptical Ian Wilson, citing pre-Christian remains found in 1955 under the Church of the Annunciation in present-day Nazareth, has managed to concede, "Such findings suggest that Nazareth may have existed in Jesus' time, but there is no doubt that it must have been a very small and insignificant place."[17]

So insignificant that Nathanael's musings in John's gospel now make more sense: "Nazareth!" he said. "Can anything good come from there?"[18]

THE CHRISTMAS STAR

Was it a comet? Asteroid? Conjunction of planets? All have been suggested to explain the Christmas star that led the wise men from the east to visit the Christ child. For astronomer Hugh Ross, one possibility is a "recurring nova."

"An easily visible nova (a star that suddenly increases in brightness and then within a few months or years grows dim) occurs about once every decade," he said. "Novae are sufficiently uncommon to catch the attention of observers as alert and well-trained as the magi must have been. However, many novae are also sufficiently unspectacular as to escape the attention of others."

Most novae explode once, but a few undergo multiple explosions separated by months or years. This, he said, could account for how Matthew says the star appeared, disappeared, and then reappeared and disappeared later.

PUZZLE 3: SLAUGHTER AT BETHLEHEM

The gospel of Matthew paints a grisly scene: Herod the Great, the king of Judea, feeling threatened by the birth of a baby whom he feared would eventually seize his throne, dispatches his troops to murder all the children under the age of two in Bethlehem. Warned by an angel, however, Joseph escapes to Egypt with Mary and Jesus. Only after Herod dies do they return to settle in Nazareth, the entire episode having fulfilled three ancient prophecies about the Messiah.[19]

The problem: there is no independent confirmation that this mass murder ever took place. There's nothing about it in the writings of Josephus or other historians. There's no archaeological support. There are no records or documents.

"Certainly an event of this magnitude would have been noticed by someone other than Matthew," I insisted. "With the complete absence of any historical or archaeological corroboration, isn't it logical to conclude that this slaughter never occurred?"

"I can see why you'd say that," McRay replied, "since today an event like that would probably be splashed all over CNN and the rest of the news media. But, you have to put yourself back in the first century and keep a few things in mind. First, Bethlehem was probably no bigger than Nazareth, so how many babies of that age would there be in a village of five hundred or six hundred people? Not thousands, not hundreds, although certainly a few.

"Second, Herod the Great was a bloodthirsty king; he killed members of his own family; he executed lots of people who he thought might challenge him. So the fact that he killed some babies in Bethlehem is not going to captivate the attention of people in the Roman world.

"And third, there was no television, no radio, no newspapers. It would have taken a long time for word of this to get out, especially from such a minor village way in the back hills of nowhere, and historians had much bigger stories to write about."

As a journalist, this was still hard to fathom. "This just wasn't much of a story?" I asked, a bit incredulous.

"I don't think it was, at least not in those days," he said. "A madman killing everybody who seems to be a potential threat to him—that was business as usual for Herod. Later, of course, as Christianity developed, this incident became more important, but I would have been surprised if this had made a big splash back then."

I had to acknowledge that from what I knew of the bloody landscape of ancient Palestine, McRay's explanation did seem reasonable. Indeed, I walked away from my interview with McRay even more convinced about the overall accuracy of the New Testament.

As Australian archaeologist Clifford Wilson said: "Those who know the facts now recognize that the New Testament must be accepted as a remarkably accurate source book."[20]

On top of that, the New Testament is further corroborated by ancient historical sources from outside the Bible. "We have better historical documentation for Jesus than for the founder of any other ancient religion," Dr. Edwin Yamauchi told me during my visit to Miami University of Ohio.

Yamauchi, who earned his doctorate in Mediterranean studies from Brandeis University, is the author of *The*

Scriptures and Archaeology and *The World of the First Christians*. When I asked him what we would be able to conclude about Jesus purely by relying on ancient non-Christian sources, he replied:

"We would know that first, Jesus was a Jewish teacher; second, many people believed that he performed healings and exorcisms; third, some people believed he was the Messiah; fourth, he was rejected by the Jewish leaders; fifth, he was crucified under Pontius Pilate in the reign of Tiberius; sixth, despite his shameful death, his followers, who believed that he was still alive, spread beyond Palestine so that there were multitudes of them in Rome by AD 64; and seventh, all kinds of people from the cities and countryside—men and women, slave and free—worshiped him as God."

One expert documented thirty-nine ancient historical sources that corroborate more than one hundred facts concerning Jesus' life, teachings, crucifixion, and resurrection. Seven secular sources and several early creeds concern the deity of Jesus, a doctrine "definitely present in the earliest church," according to Dr. Gary Habermas, author of *The Historical Jesus*.[21]

Finally, my questions about whether the New Testament has been reliably transmitted through the centuries to the present time were answered by Dr. Bruce Metzger, professor emeritus of Princeton Theological Seminary. He told me that there is an unprecedented number of New Testament manuscripts and that they can be dated extremely close to the original writings. The modern New Testament is 99.5 percent free of textual discrepancies, with no major Christian doctrines in doubt. Further, the criteria used by the early church to determine which books should be considered authoritative have ensured that we possess the very best records about Jesus.

Those records are unambiguous in declaring that the child in the manger was the Son of God. But was he able to back up that claim? I knew there was a Christian intellectual named D. A. Carson who could help me determine if Jesus fulfilled the attributes of God.

3

THE PROFILE EVIDENCE:
DID JESUS FULFILL THE
ATTRIBUTES OF GOD?

Shortly after eight student nurses were murdered in a Chicago apartment, the trembling lone survivor huddled with a police sketch artist and described in detail the killer she had seen from her secret vantage point beneath a bed.

Quickly the drawing was flashed around the city—to police officers, to hospitals, to transit stations, to the airport. Soon an emergency room physician called detectives to say he was treating a man who looked suspiciously like the flinty-eyed fugitive depicted in the sketch.

That's how police arrested a drifter named Richard Speck, who was promptly convicted of the heinous slayings and ended up dying in prison thirty years later.[22]

Ever since Scotland Yard first turned a witness's recollections into a sketch of a murder suspect in 1889, forensic artists have played an important role in law enforcement. Today more than three hundred sketch artists work with U.S. police agencies.

Oddly enough, the concept of an artist's drawing can provide a rough analogy that can help us in our quest for the truth about the identity of the Christmas child.

Here's how: The Old Testament provides numerous details about God that sketch out in great specificity what he's like. For instance, God is described as omnipresent, or existing everywhere in the universe; as omniscient, or knowing everything that can be known throughout eternity; as omnipotent, or all-powerful; as eternal, or being both beyond time and the source of all time; and as immutable, or unchanging in his attributes. He's loving, he's holy, he's righteous, he's wise, he's just.

Now, Jesus claims to be the Son of God. But does he fulfill these characteristics of deity? In other words, if we examine Jesus carefully, does his likeness closely match the sketch of God that we find elsewhere in the Bible? If it doesn't, we can conclude that his claim to being God is false.

This is an extremely complex and mind-stretching issue. For example, when Jesus was delivering the Sermon on the Mount on a hillside outside Capernaum, he wasn't simultaneously standing on Main Street of Jericho, so in what sense could he be called omnipresent? How can he be called omniscient if he readily admits in Mark 13:32 that he doesn't know everything about the future? If he's eternal, why does Colossians 1:15 call him "the firstborn over all creation"?

On the surface these issues seem to suggest that Jesus doesn't resemble the sketch of God. Nevertheless, I've learned over the years that initial impressions can be deceiving. That's why I was glad I would be able to discuss these issues with Dr. D. A. Carson, the theologian who has emerged in recent years as one of the most distinguished thinkers in Christianity.

INTERVIEW: DONALD A. CARSON, PHD

D. A. Carson, a research professor of New Testament at Trinity Evangelical Divinity School, has written or edited more than forty books, including *The Sermon on the*

Mount, Exegetical Fallacies, The Gospel According to John, and his award-winning *The Gagging of God.* He earned his doctorate in New Testament at prestigious Cambridge University and taught at three other colleges and seminaries before joining Trinity in 1978.

My initial question centered on why Carson thinks Jesus is God in the first place. "What did he say or do," I asked, "that convinces you that he is divine?" I wasn't sure how he would respond, although I anticipated he would focus on Jesus' supernatural feats. I was wrong.

"One could point to such things as his miracles," Carson said, "but other people have done miracles, so while this may be indicative, it's not decisive. Of course, the resurrection was the ultimate vindication of his identity. But of the many things he did, one of the most striking to me is his forgiving of sin."

"Really?" I said. "How so?"

"The point is, if you do something against me, I have the right to forgive you. However, if you do something against me and somebody else comes along and says, 'I forgive you,' what kind of cheek is that? The only person who can say that sort of thing meaningfully is God himself, because sin, even if it is against other people, is first and foremost a defiance of God and his laws.

"When David sinned by committing adultery and arranging the death of the woman's husband, he ultimately says to God in Psalm 51, 'Against you only have I sinned and done this evil in your sight.' He recognized that although he had wronged people, in the end he had sinned against the God who made him in his image, and God needed to forgive him.

"So along comes Jesus and says to sinners, 'I forgive you.' The Jews immediately recognize the blasphemy of this. They react by saying, 'Who can forgive sins but God alone?' To my mind, that is one of the most striking things Jesus did."

"Not only did Jesus forgive sin," I observed, "but he asserted that he himself was without sin. And certainly sinlessness is an attribute of deity."

"Yes," he replied. "Historically in the West, people considered most holy have also been the most conscious of their own failures and sins. They are people who are aware of their shortcomings and lusts and resentments, and they're fighting them honestly by the grace of God. In fact, they're fighting them so well that others take notice and say, 'There is a holy man or woman.'

"But along comes Jesus, who can say with a straight face, 'Which of you can convict me of sin?' If I said that, my wife and children and all who know me would be glad to stand up and testify, whereas no one could with respect to Christ."

Although moral perfection and the forgiveness of sin are undoubtedly characteristics of deity, there are several additional attributes that Jesus must fulfill if he is to match the sketch of God. It was time to progress to those. After having started by lobbing softballs at Carson, I got ready to throw some curves.

MYSTERY OF THE INCARNATION

Using some notes I had brought along, I hit Carson in rapid-fire succession with some of the biggest obstacles to Jesus' claim of deity.

"Dr. Carson, how in the world could Jesus be omni-present if he couldn't be in two places at once?" I asked. "How could he be omniscient when he says, 'Not even the Son of Man knows the hour of his return'? How could he be omnipotent when the gospels plainly tell us that he was unable to do many miracles in his hometown?"

Pointing my pen at him for emphasis, I concluded by saying, "Let's admit it: the Bible itself seems to argue against Jesus being God."

While Carson didn't flinch, he did concede that these questions have no simple answers. After all, they strike at the very heart of the incarnation, which is what Christ-mas is all about—God becoming man, spirit taking on flesh, the infinite entering the finite, the eternal becom-ing time-bound. It's a doctrine that has kept theologians busy for centuries. And that's where Carson chose to start his answer: by going back to the way scholars have tried to respond to these matters through the years.

"Historically, there have been two or three approaches to this," he began, sounding a bit as if he were begin-ning a classroom lecture.

"For example, at the end of the last century, the great theologian Benjamin Warfield worked through the gospels and ascribed various bits either to Christ's humanity or to his deity. When Jesus does something that's a reflection of him being God, that's ascribed to Christ's deity. When there's something reflecting his limitations or finiteness or his humanness—for example, his tears; does God cry?—that's ascribed to his humanity."

That explanation was fraught with problems, it seemed to me. "If you do that, wouldn't you end up with a schiz-ophrenic Jesus?" I asked.

"It's easy to slip into that unwittingly," he replied. "All the confessional statements have insisted that both Jesus' humanity and his deity remained distinct, yet they combined in one person. So you want to avoid a solution in which there are essentially two minds—sort of a Jesus human mind and a Christ heavenly mind. However, this is one kind of solution, and there may be something to it.

"The other kind of solution is some form of *kenosis*, which means 'emptying.' This spins out of Philippians 2, where Paul tells us that Jesus, 'being in the form of God, did not think equality with God was something to be exploited'—that's the way it should be translated—'but emptied himself.' He became a nobody."

That seemed a little ambiguous to me. "Can you be more explicit?" I asked. "What exactly did he empty himself of?"

Apparently, I had put my finger on the issue. "Ah, that's the question," Carson replied with a nod. "Through the centuries, people have given various answers to that. For instance, did he empty himself of his deity? Well, then he would no longer be God.

"Did he empty himself of the attributes of his deity? I have a problem with that too, because it's difficult to separate attributes from reality. If you have an animal that looks like a horse, smells like a horse, walks like a horse, and has all the attributes of a horse, you've got a horse. So I don't know what it means for God to empty himself of his attributes and still be God.

"Some have said, 'He didn't empty himself of his attributes, but he emptied himself of the use of his attributes'—a self-limiting type of thing. That's getting closer, although there are times when that was not what he was doing—he was forgiving sins the way only God can, which is an attribute of deity.

"Others go further by saying, 'He emptied himself of the independent use of his attributes.' That is, he functioned like God when his heavenly Father gave him explicit sanction to do so. Now, that's much closer. The difficulty is that there is a sense in which the eternal Son has always acted in line with his Father's commandments. You don't want to lose that, even in eternity past. But it's getting closer."

I sensed we were somewhere in the vicinity of the bull's-eye, but I wasn't sure we were going to get more accurate. That seemed to be Carson's sentiment, too.

"Strictly speaking," he said, "Philippians 2 does not tell us precisely what the eternal Son emptied himself of. He emptied himself; he became a nobody. Some kind of emptying is at issue, but let's be frank—you're talking about the incarnation, one of the central mysteries of the Christian faith.

"You're dealing with formless, bodiless, omniscient, omnipresent, omnipotent Spirit and finite, touchable, physical, time-bound creatures. For one to become the other inevitably binds you up in mysteries.

"So part of Christian theology has been concerned not with 'explaining it all away' but with trying to take the biblical evidence and, retaining all of it fairly, finding ways of synthesis that are rationally coherent, even if they're not exhaustively explanatory."

That was a sophisticated way of saying that theologians can come up with explanations that seem to make sense, even though they might not be able to explain every nuance about the incarnation. In a way, that seemed logical. If the incarnation is true, it's not surprising that finite minds couldn't totally comprehend it.

It seemed to me that some sort of voluntary "emptying" of Jesus' independent use of his attributes was reasonable in explaining why he generally didn't exhibit the "omnis"— omniscience, omnipotence, and omnipresence—in his earthly existence, even though the New Testament clearly states that all these qualities are ultimately true of him.

That, however, was only part of the problem. I flipped to the next page of my notes and began another line of questioning about a biblical passage that seemed to directly contradict Jesus' claim to being God.

CREATOR OR CREATED?

Part of the sketch that Jesus must match is that God is an uncreated being who has existed from eternity past. Isaiah 57:15 describes God as "he who lives forever." But, I said to Carson, there are some verses that seem to strongly suggest that Jesus was a created being who first came into existence when he was born in Bethlehem.

"For instance," I said, "John 3:16 calls Jesus the 'begotten' Son of God, and Colossians 1:15 says he was the 'firstborn over all creation.' Don't they clearly imply that Jesus was created, as opposed to being the Creator?"

One of Carson's areas of expertise is Greek grammar, which he called upon in responding to both of those verses.

"Let's take John 3:16," he said. "It's the King James Version that translates the Greek with the words 'his only begotten Son.' Those who consider this the correct rendering usually bind that up with the incarnation itself—that is, his begetting in the Virgin Mary. But in fact, that's not what the word in Greek means.

"It really means 'unique one.' The way it was usually used in the first century is 'unique and beloved.' So John 3:16 is simply saying that Jesus is the unique and beloved Son—or as the New International Version translates it, 'the one and only Son'—rather than saying that he's ontologically begotten in time."

WHO DOES JESUS THINK HE IS?

Did the Christmas child grow up to consider himself the Messiah and Son of God, or did he think of himself as merely a rabbi or prophet? Based on the very earliest traditions about Jesus, which are unquestionably safe from legendary development, Dr. Ben Witherington III, author of *The Christology of Jesus*, told me: "Did Jesus believe he was the Son of God, the anointed one of God? The answer is yes. Did he see himself as the Son of Man? The answer is yes. Did he see himself as the final Messiah? Yes, that's the way he viewed himself. Did he believe that anyone less than God could save the world? No, I don't believe he did."

"That only explains that one passage," I pointed out.

"Okay, let's look at the Colossians verse, which uses the term *firstborn*. The vast majority of commentators, whether conservative or liberal, recognize that in the Old Testament the firstborn, because of the laws of succession, normally received the lion's share of the estate, or the firstborn would become king in the case of a royal family. The firstborn therefore was the one ultimately with all the rights of the father.

"By the second century before Christ, there are places where the word no longer has any notion of actual begetting or of being born first but carries the idea of the authority that comes with the position of being the rightful heir. That's the way it applies to Jesus, as virtually all scholars admit. In light of that, the very expression 'firstborn' is slightly misleading."

"What would be a better translation?" I asked.

"I think 'supreme heir' would be more appropriate," he responded.

While that would explain the Colossians passage, Carson went even further, with one last point.

"If you're going to quote Colossians 1:15, you have to keep it in context by going on to Colossians 2:9, where the very same author stresses, 'For in Christ all the fullness of the Deity lives in bodily form.' The author wouldn't contradict himself. So the term *firstborn* cannot exclude Jesus' eternality, since that is part of what it means to possess the fullness of the divine."

For me, that nailed it.

MATCHING THE SKETCH OF GOD

Carson and I talked, sometimes in animated tones, for two hours, filling more tapes than would fit in this chapter. I found his answers to be well reasoned and theologically sound. In the end, however, how the incarnation works—how Spirit takes on flesh—remained a mind-boggling concept.

Even so, according to the Bible, the fact that it did occur is not in any doubt. Every attribute of God, says the New Testament, is ultimately found in the Christmas child who grew up to live a life unlike any other:

- Omniscience? In John 16:30 the apostle John affirms of Jesus, "Now we can see that you know all things."
- Omnipresence? Jesus said in Matthew 28:20, "Surely I am with you always, to the very end of the age" and in Matthew 18:20, "Where two or three come together in my name, there am I with them."
- Omnipotence? "All authority in heaven and on earth has been given to me," Jesus said in Matthew 28:18.
- Eternality? John 1:1 declares of Jesus, "In the beginning was the Word, and the Word was with God, and the Word was God."
- Immutability? Hebrews 13:8 says, "Jesus Christ is the same yesterday and today and forever."

Also, the Old Testament paints a portrait of God by using such titles and descriptions as Alpha and Omega, Lord, Savior, King, Judge, Light, Rock, Redeemer, Shepherd, Creator, giver of life, forgiver of sin, and speaker with divine authority. It's fascinating to note that in the New Testament each and every one is applied to Jesus.[23]

Jesus said it all in John 14:7: "If you really knew me, you would know my Father as well." Loose translation: "When you look at the sketch of God from the Old Testament, you will see a likeness of me."

4

THE FINGERPRINT EVIDENCE: DID JESUS — AND JESUS ALONE — MATCH THE IDENTITY OF THE MESSIAH?

It was an uneventful Saturday at the Hiller home in Chicago. Clarence Hiller spent the afternoon painting the trim on the outside of his two-story house on West 104th Street. By early evening he and his family had retired to bed. However, what happened next would change criminal law in America forever.

The Hillers woke in the early morning hours of September 19, 1910, and became suspicious that a gaslight near their daughter's bedroom had gone out. Clarence went to investigate. His wife heard a quick succession of sounds: a scuffle, two men tumbling down the stairs, two gunshots, and the slamming of the front door. She emerged to find Clarence dead at the foot of the stairs.

Police arrested Thomas Jennings, a convicted burglar, less than a mile away. There was blood on his clothes and his left arm had been injured—both, he said, from falling on a streetcar. In his pocket they found the same kind of gun that had been used to shoot Clarence Hiller, but they couldn't determine if it was the murder weapon.

Knowing they needed more to convict Jennings, detectives scoured the inside of Hiller's home in a search for additional clues. One fact soon became obvious: the killer had entered through a rear kitchen window. Detectives went outside—and there, next to that window, forever imprinted in the white paint that the murder victim himself had so carefully applied to a railing only hours before his death, they found four clear fingerprints from someone's left hand.

Fingerprint evidence was a new concept at the time, and it had never been used to convict anyone of murder in the United States. Despite strong objections by defense attorneys that such evidence was unscientific, four officers testified that the fingerprints in the paint perfectly matched those of Thomas Jennings—and him alone. The jury found Jennings guilty, and he was later hanged.[24]

The premise behind fingerprint evidence is simple: each individual has unique ridges on his or her fingers. When a print found on an object matches the pattern of ridges on a person's finger, investigators can conclude with confidence that this specific individual has touched that object.

Okay, but what has this got to do with the identity of the Christmas child? Simply this: There is another kind of evidence that's analogous to fingerprints and establishes to an astounding degree of certainty that Jesus is indeed the Messiah of Israel and the world.

In the Jewish Scriptures, which Christians call the Old Testament, there are several dozen major prophecies about the coming of the Messiah, whom God would send to redeem his people. In effect, these predictions formed a figurative fingerprint that only the Anointed One would be able to match. This way, the Israelites could rule out any impostors and validate the credentials of the authentic Messiah.

The Greek word for "Messiah" is *Christ*. But was the baby in the manger really the Christ? Did he miraculously fulfill these predictions that were written hundreds of years before he was born? And how do we know he was the only individual throughout history who fit the prophetic fingerprint?

There are plenty of scholars I could have asked about this topic. However, I wanted to interview someone for whom this was more than just an abstract academic exercise, and that took me to a very unlikely setting in southern California.

INTERVIEW: LOUIS S. LAPIDES, MDIV, THM

Usually a church would be a natural location in which to question someone about a biblical issue. But there was something different about sitting down with Pastor Louis Lapides in the sanctuary of his congregation on the morning after Sunday worship services. This setting of pews and stained glass was not where you would expect to find a nice Jewish boy from Newark, New Jersey.

Yet that's Lapides' background. For someone with his heritage, the question of whether Jesus is the long-anticipated Messiah goes beyond theory. It's intensely personal, and I had sought out Lapides so I could hear the story of his own investigation of this critical issue.

Lapides earned a bachelor's degree in theology from Dallas Baptist University, as well as a master of divinity and a master of theology degree in Old Testament and Semitics from Talbot Theological Seminary. He served for a decade with Chosen People Ministries, talking about Jesus to Jewish college students. He has taught in the Bible department of Biola University and is the former president of a national network of fifteen messianic congregations.

Slender and bespectacled, Lapides is soft-spoken but has a quick smile and ready laugh. He was upbeat and polite as he ushered me to a chair near the front of Beth Ariel Fellowship in Sherman Oaks, California. I didn't want to begin by debating biblical nuances; instead I started by inviting Lapides to tell me the story of his spiritual journey.

"As you know, I came from a Jewish family," he began. "I attended a conservative Jewish synagogue for seven years in preparation for bar mitzvah. Although we considered those studies to be very important, our family's faith didn't affect our everyday life very much. We didn't stop work on the Sabbath; we didn't have a kosher home."

When I interjected to ask what his parents had taught him about the Messiah, Lapides' answer was crisp. "It never came up," he said matter-of-factly.

I was incredulous. "You're saying it wasn't even discussed?" I asked.

"Never," he reiterated. "I don't even remember it being an issue in Hebrew school."

This was amazing to me. "How about Jesus?" I asked. "Was he ever talked about? Was his name used?"

"Only derogatorily!" Lapides quipped. "Basically, he was never discussed. My impressions of Jesus came from seeing Catholic churches: there was the cross, the crown of thorns, the pierced side, the blood coming from his head. It didn't make any sense to me. Why would you worship a man on a cross with nails in his hands and his feet? I never once thought Jesus had any connection to the Jewish people. I just thought he was a god of the Gentiles."

I suspected that Lapides' attitudes toward Christians had gone beyond mere confusion over their beliefs. "Did you believe Christians were at the root of anti-Semitism?" I asked.

"Gentiles were looked upon as synonymous with Christians, and we were taught to be cautious because there could be anti-Semitism among the Gentiles," he said, sounding diplomatic.

I pursued the issue further. "Would you say you developed some negative attitudes toward Christians?"

This time he didn't mince words. "Yes, actually I did," he said. "In fact, later when the New Testament was first presented to me, I sincerely thought it was going to basically be a handbook on anti-Semitism: how to hate Jews, how to kill Jews, how to massacre them. I thought the American Nazi Party would have been very comfortable using it as a guidebook."

I shook my head, saddened at the thought of how many other Jewish children have grown up thinking of Christians as their enemies.

A SPIRITUAL QUEST BEGINS

Lapides said several incidents dimmed his allegiance to Judaism as he was growing up. Curious about the details, I asked him to elaborate, and he immediately turned to what was clearly the most heartrending episode of his life.

"My parents got divorced when I was seventeen," he said—and surprisingly, even after all these years I could still detect hurt in his voice. "That really put a stake in any religious heart I may have had. I wondered, Where does

God come in? Why didn't they go to a rabbi for counseling? What good is religion if it can't help people in a practical way? It sure couldn't keep my parents together. When they split up, part of me split as well.

"On top of that, in Judaism I didn't feel as if I had a personal relationship with God. I had a lot of beautiful ceremonies and traditions, but he was the distant and detached God of Mount Sinai who said, 'Here are the rules—you live by them, you'll be okay; I'll see you later.' And there I was, an adolescent with raging hormones, wondering, Does God relate to my struggles? Does he care about me as an individual? Well, not in any way I could see."

The divorce prompted an era of rebellion. Consumed with music and influenced by the writings of Jack Kerouac and Timothy Leary, he spent too much time in Greenwich Village coffeehouses to go to college—making him vulnerable to the draft. By 1967 he found himself in Vietnam.

"It was a very dark period. I witnessed suffering. I saw body bags; I saw the devastation from war. And I encountered anti-Semitism among some of the GIs. A few of them from the South even burned a cross one night. I probably wanted to distance myself from my Jewish identity—maybe that's why I began delving into eastern religions."

Lapides read books on eastern philosophies and visited Buddhist temples while in Japan. "I was extremely bothered by the evil I had seen, and I was trying to figure out how faith can deal with it," he told me. "I used to say, 'If there's a God, I don't care if I find him on Mount Sinai or Mount Fuji. I'll take him either way.'"

He survived Vietnam, returning home with a new-found taste for marijuana and plans to become a Buddhist priest. He tried to live an ascetic lifestyle of self-denial in an effort to work off the bad karma for the misdeeds of his past, but soon he realized he'd never be able to make up for all his wrongs.

Following a period of depression and experimentation with LSD, he decided to move to California for a new start. His spiritual quest continued, but nothing seemed to satisfy him. He even accompanied friends to meetings that had satanic undercurrents.

"I would watch and think, Something is going on here, but it's not good," he said. "In the midst of my drug-crazed world, I told my friends I believed there's a power of evil that's beyond me, that can work in me, that exists as an entity. I had seen enough evil in my life to believe that."

He looked at me with an ironic smile. "I guess I accepted Satan's existence," he said, "before I accepted God's."

"I Can't Believe in Jesus"

It was 1969. Lapides' curiosity prompted him to visit Sunset Strip to gawk at an evangelist who had chained himself to an eight-foot cross to protest his eviction from his storefront ministry. There on the sidewalk Lapides encountered some Christians who engaged him in an impromptu spiritual debate.

A bit cocky, he started throwing Eastern philosophy at them. "There is no God out there," he said, gesturing toward the heavens. "We're God. I'm God. You're God. You just have to realize it."

"Well, if you're God, why don't you create a rock?" one person replied. "Just make something appear. That's what God does."

In his drug-addled mind Lapides imagined he was holding a rock. "Yeah, well, here's a rock," he said, extending his empty hand.

The Christian scoffed. "That's the difference between you and the true God," he said. "When God creates something, everyone can see it. It's objective, not subjective."

That registered with Lapides. After thinking about it for a while, he said to himself, *If I find God, he's got to be objective. I'm through with this Eastern philosophy that says it's all in my mind and that I can create my own reality. God has to be an objective reality if he's going to have any meaning beyond my own imagination.*

When one of the Christians brought up the name of Jesus, Lapides tried to fend him off with his stock answer. "I'm Jewish," he said. "I can't believe in Jesus."

A pastor spoke up. "Do you know of the prophecies about the Messiah?" he asked.

Lapides was taken off guard. "Prophecies?" he said. "I've never heard of them."

The minister startled Lapides by referring to some of the Old Testament predictions. *Wait a minute!* Lapides thought. *Those are my Jewish Scriptures he's quoting! How could Jesus be in there?*

When the pastor offered him a Bible, Lapides was skeptical. "Is the New Testament in there?" he asked. The pastor nodded. "Okay, I'll read the Old Testament, but I'm not going to open up the other one," Lapides told him.

He was taken aback by the minister's response. "Fine," said the pastor. "Just read the Old Testament and ask the

God of Abraham, Isaac, and Jacob—the God of Israel—
to show you if Jesus is the Messiah. Because he *is* your
Messiah. He came to the Jewish people initially, and then
he was also the Savior of the world."

To Lapides, this was new—and astonishing—information. So he went back to his apartment, opened the
Old Testament to its first book, Genesis, and went hunt-
ing for Jesus among words that had been written hundreds
of years before the first-century carpenter had ever been
born in Bethlehem.

"PIERCED FOR OUR TRANSGRESSIONS"

"Pretty soon," Lapides told me, "I was reading the Old
Testament every day and seeing one prophecy after another.
For instance, Deuteronomy talked about a prophet greater
than Moses who will come and whom we should listen to.
I thought, Who can be greater than Moses? It sounded like
the Messiah—someone as great and as respected as Moses
but a greater teacher and a greater authority. I grabbed
ahold of that and went searching for him."

As Lapides progressed through the Scriptures, he was
stopped cold by Isaiah 53. With clarity and specificity,
in a haunting prediction wrapped in exquisite poetry, here
was the picture of a Messiah who would suffer and die for
the sins of Israel and the world—all written more than
seven hundred years before Jesus walked the earth.

> He was despised and rejected by men,
>   a man of sorrows, and familiar with suffering.
> Like one from whom men hide their faces
>   he was despised, and we esteemed him not.

Surely he took up our infirmities
  and carried our sorrows,
yet we considered him stricken by God,
  smitten by him, and afflicted.
But he was pierced for our transgressions,
  he was crushed for our iniquities;
the punishment that brought us peace was upon him,
  and by his wounds we are healed.
We all, like sheep, have gone astray,
  each of us has turned to his own way;
and the Lord has laid on him
  the iniquity of us all.

He was oppressed and afflicted,
  yet he did not open his mouth;
he was led like a lamb to the slaughter,
  and as a sheep before her shearers is silent,
  so he did not open his mouth.
By oppression and judgment he was taken away.
  And who can speak of his descendants?
For he was cut off from the land of the living;
  for the transgression of my people he was stricken.
He was assigned a grave with the wicked,
  and with the rich in his death,
though he had done no violence,
nor was any deceit in his mouth....

For he bore the sin of many,
  and made intercession for the transgressors.[25]

Instantly Lapides recognized the portrait: this was Jesus of Nazareth! Now he was beginning to understand the paintings he had seen in the Catholic churches he had passed as a child: the suffering Jesus, the crucified Jesus, the Jesus who he now realized had been "pierced for our transgressions" as he "bore the sin of many."

As Jews in the Old Testament sought to atone for their sins through a system of animal sacrifices, here was Jesus, the ultimate sacrificial lamb of God, who paid for sin once and for all. Here was the personification of God's plan of redemption.

So breathtaking was this discovery that Lapides could only come to one conclusion: it was a fraud! He believed that Christians had rewritten the Old Testament and twisted Isaiah's words to make it sound as if the prophet had been foreshadowing Jesus.

Lapides set out to expose the deception. "I asked my stepmother to send me a Jewish Bible so I could check it out myself," he told me. "She did, and guess what? I found that it said the same thing! Now I really had to deal with it."

THE JEWISHNESS OF JESUS

Over and over Lapides would come upon prophecies in the Old Testament—more than four dozen major predictions in all. Isaiah revealed the manner of the Messiah's birth (of a virgin); Micah pinpointed the place of his birth (Bethlehem); Genesis and Jeremiah specified his ancestry (a descendent of Abraham, Isaac, and Jacob, from the tribe of Judah, the house of David); the Psalms foretold his betrayal, his accusation by false witnesses, his manner of death (pierced in the hands and feet, although crucifixion hadn't been invented yet), and his resurrection (he would not decay but would ascend on high); and on and on.[26] Each one chipped away at Lapides' skepticism until he was finally willing to take a drastic step.

"I decided to open the New Testament and just read the first page," he said. "With trepidation I slowly turned to Matthew as I looked up to heaven, waiting for the lightning bolt to strike!"

Matthew's initial words leaped off the page: "A record of the genealogy of Jesus Christ the son of David, the son of Abraham . . ."

Lapides' eyes widened as he recalled the moment he first read that sentence. "I thought, Wow! Son of Abraham, son of David—it was all fitting together! I went to the birth narratives and thought, Look at this! Matthew is quoting from Isaiah 7:14: 'The virgin will be with child and will give birth to a son.' And then I saw him quoting from the prophet Jeremiah. I sat there thinking, You know, this is about Jewish people. Where do the Gentiles come in? What's going on here?

"I couldn't put it down. I read through the rest of the Gospels, and I realized this wasn't a handbook for the American Nazi Party; it was an interaction between Jesus and the Jewish community. I got to the book of Acts and—this was incredible!—they were trying to figure out how the Jews could bring the story of Jesus to the Gentiles. Talk about role reversal!"

So convincing were the fulfilled prophecies that Lapides started telling people that he thought Jesus was the Messiah. At the time, this was merely an intellectual possibility to him, yet its implications were deeply troubling.

"I realized that if I were to accept Jesus into my life, there would have to be some significant changes in the way I was living," he explained. "I'd have to deal with the drugs, the sex, and so forth. I didn't understand that

God would help me make those changes; I thought I had to clean up my life on my own."

EPIPHANY IN THE DESERT

Lapides and some friends headed into the Mojave Desert for a getaway. Spiritually he was feeling conflicted. Sitting among the desert scrub, he recalled the words someone had spoken to him on Sunset Strip: "You're either on God's side or on Satan's side."

He believed in the embodiment of evil—and that's not whose side he wanted to be on. So Lapides prayed, "God, I've got to come to the end of this struggle. I have to know beyond a shadow of a doubt that Jesus is the Messiah. I need to know that you, as the God of Israel, want me to believe this."

As he related the story to me, Lapides hesitated, unsure how to put into words what happened next. A few moments passed. Then he told me, "The best I can put together out of that experience is that God objectively spoke to my heart. He convinced me, experientially, that he exists. And at that point, out in the desert, in my heart I said, 'God, I accept Jesus into my life. I don't understand what I'm supposed to do with him, but I want him. I've pretty much made a mess of my life; I need you to change me.'"

And God began to do that in a process that continues to this day. "My friends knew my life had changed, and they couldn't understand it," he said. "They'd say, 'Something happened to you in the desert. You don't want to do drugs anymore. There's something different about you.'

"I would say, 'Well, I can't explain what happened. All I know is that there's someone in my life, and it's someone who's holy, who's righteous, who's a source of positive thoughts about life—and I just feel whole.'"

That last word, it seemed, said everything. *"Whole,"* he emphasized to me, "in a way I had never felt before."

Later, through a remarkable string of circumstances, Lapides' prayer for a wife was answered when he met Deborah, who was also Jewish and a follower of Jesus. She took him to her church—the same one, it turned out, that was pastored by the minister who many months earlier on Sunset Strip had challenged Lapides to read the Old Testament.

Lapides laughed. "I'll tell you what—his jaw dropped open when he saw me walk into the church!"

He married Deborah a year after they met. Since then she has given birth to two sons. And together they've given birth to Beth Ariel Fellowship, a home for Jews and Gentiles who also are finding wholeness in Christ.

RESPONDING TO OBJECTIONS

Lapides' story was moving to me, and I paused for a few moments to let it soak in. Still, it raised some questions. "If the prophecies were so obvious to you and pointed so unquestionably toward Jesus," I asked, "then why don't more Jews accept him as their Messiah?"

"In my case, I took the time to read them," he replied. "Oddly enough, even though the Jewish people are known for having high intellects, in this area there's a lot of ignorance. Plus you have countermissionary organizations that hold seminars in synagogues to try to disprove the messianic prophecies. Jewish people hear them and use them as an excuse for not exploring the prophecies personally. They'll say, 'The rabbi told me there's nothing to this.'

"I'll ask them, 'Do you think the rabbi just brought up an objection that Christianity has never heard before? I mean, scholars have been working on this for hundreds of years! There's great literature out there and powerful Christian answers to those challenges.' If they're interested, I help them go further."

I wondered about the ostracism a Jewish person faces if he or she becomes a Christian. "That's definitely a factor," he said. "Some people won't let the messianic prophecies grab them, because they're afraid of the repercussions—potential rejection by their family and the Jewish community. That's not easy to face. Believe me, I know."

Even so, some of the challenges to the prophecies sound pretty convincing when a person first hears them. So one by one I posed the most common objections to Lapides to see how he would respond.

1. THE COINCIDENCE ARGUMENT

First, I asked Lapides whether it's possible that Jesus merely fulfilled the prophecies by accident. Maybe he's just one of many throughout history who have coincidentally fit the prophetic fingerprint.

"Not a chance," came his response. "The odds are so astronomical that they rule that out. Someone estimated that the probability of just eight prophecies being fulfilled is one chance in one hundred million billion. That number is millions of times greater than the total number of people who've ever walked the planet!

"He calculated that if you took this number of silver dollars they would cover the state of Texas to a depth of two feet. If you marked one silver dollar among them and then had a blindfolded person wander the whole state and bend down to pick up one coin, what would be the odds he'd choose the one that had been marked?"

With that he answered his own question: "The same odds that anybody in history could have fulfilled just eight of the prophecies."

I had studied this same statistical analysis by mathematician Peter W. Stoner when I was investigating the messianic prophecies for myself. Stoner also estimated that the probability of fulfilling forty-eight prophecies was one chance in a trillion, trillion, trillion, trillion, trillion, trillion, trillion, trillion, trillion, trillion, trillion, trillion, trillion![27]

Our minds can't comprehend a number that big. This is a staggering statistic that's equal to the number of minuscule atoms in a trillion, trillion, trillion, trillion, billion universes the size of our universe!

"The odds alone say it would be impossible for anyone to fulfill the Old Testament prophecies," Lapides concluded. "Yet Jesus—and only Jesus throughout all of history—managed to do it."

The words of the apostle Peter popped into my head: "But the things which God announced beforehand by the mouth of all the prophets, that His Christ should suffer, He has thus fulfilled."[28]

2. THE ALTERED GOSPEL ARGUMENT

I painted another scenario for Lapides, asking, "Isn't it possible that the gospel writers fabricated details to make it appear that Jesus fulfilled the prophecies?

"For example," I said, "the prophecies say the Messiah's bones would remain unbroken, so maybe John invented the story about the Romans breaking the legs of the two thieves being crucified with Jesus, and not breaking his legs. And the prophecies talk about betrayal for thirty pieces of silver, so maybe Matthew played fast and loose with the facts and said, yeah, Judas sold out Jesus for that same amount."

But that objection didn't fly any further than the previous one. "In God's wisdom, he created checks and balances both inside and outside the Christian community," Lapides explained. "When the Gospels were being circulated, there were people living who had been around when all these things happened. Someone would have said to Matthew, 'You know it didn't happen that way. We're trying to communicate a life of righteousness and truth, so don't taint it with a lie.'

"Besides," he added, "why would Matthew have fabricated fulfilled prophecies and then be willing to be put to death for following someone who he secretly knew was really not the Messiah? That wouldn't make any sense.

"What's more, the Jewish community would have jumped on any opportunity to discredit the Gospels by pointing out falsehoods. They would have said, 'I was there, and Jesus' bones *were* broken by the Romans during the crucifixion,'" Lapides said. "But even though the Jewish Talmud refers to Jesus in derogatory ways, it never once makes the claim that the fulfillment of prophecies was falsified. Not one time."

3. THE INTENTIONAL FULFILLMENT ARGUMENT

Some skeptics have asserted that Jesus merely maneuvered his life in a way to fulfill the prophecies. "Couldn't he have read in Zechariah that the Messiah would ride a donkey into Jerusalem, and then arrange to do exactly that?" I asked.

"For a few of the prophecies, yes, that's certainly conceivable," he said. "But there are many others for which this just wouldn't have been possible.

"For instance, how would he control the fact that the Sanhedrin offered Judas thirty pieces of silver to betray him? How could he arrange for his ancestry, or the place of his birth, or his method of execution, or that soldiers gambled for his clothing, or that his legs remained unbroken on the cross? How would he arrange to perform miracles in front of skeptics? How would he arrange for his resurrection? And how would he arrange to be born when he was?"

That last comment piqued my curiosity. "What do you mean by when he was born?" I asked.

"When you interpret Daniel 9:24–26, it foretells that the Messiah would appear a certain length of time after King Artaxerxes I issued a decree for the Jewish people to go from Persia to rebuild the walls in Jerusalem," Lapides replied.

He leaned forward to deliver the clincher: "That puts the anticipated appearance of the Messiah at the exact moment in history when Jesus showed up," he said. "Certainly that's nothing he could have prearranged."[29]

4. THE CONTEXT ARGUMENT

One other objection needed to be addressed: Were the passages that Christians identify as messianic prophecies really intended to point to the coming of the Anointed

One, or do Christians rip them out of context and mis-interpret them?

Lapides sighed. "You know, I go through the books that people write to try to tear down what we believe. That's not fun to do, but I spend the time to look at each objection individually and then to research the context and the wording in the original language," he said. "And every single time, the prophecies have stood up and shown themselves to be true.

PROPHECY OF THE VIRGIN BIRTH

Hundreds of years before Jesus was born in Bethle-hem, Isaiah 7:14 foretold: "Therefore the Lord himself will give you a sign: The virgin will be with child and will give birth to a son, and will call him Immanuel." Crit-ics, however, have said this is a mistranslation. They claim the Hebrew word used in this prophecy, *almah*, merely means "young woman," and that *bethulah* would have been used if the idea of virginity were intended.

But researcher Glenn Miller told me that the latest and most detailed linguistic studies show *bethulah* could refer to a widow or divorced woman who was not a virgin. *Almah* is never used of a non-virgin. Says Miller: "If any notion of virginity were intended—even as only an 'impli-cation'—*almah* was the best/only word to do that job."

"So here's my challenge to skeptics: Don't accept my word for it, but don't accept your rabbi's either. Spend the time to research it yourself. Today nobody can say, 'There's no information.' There are plenty of books out there to help you.[30]

"And one more thing: sincerely ask God to show you whether or not Jesus is the Messiah. That's what I did—and without any coaching it became clear to me who fit the fingerprint of the Messiah."

"EVERYTHING MUST BE FULFILLED ..."

I appreciated the way Lapides had responded to the objections, but ultimately it was the story of his spiritual journey that kept replaying in my mind as I flew back to Chicago that night. I reflected on how many times I had encountered similar stories, especially among successful and thoughtful Jewish people who had specifically set out to refute Jesus' messianic claims.

I thought about Stan Telchin, the East Coast businessman who had embarked on a quest to expose the "cult" of Christianity after his daughter went away to college and received *Y'shua* (Jesus) as her Messiah. He was astonished to find that his investigation led him—and his wife and second daughter—to the same Messiah. He later became a Christian minister, and his book that recounts his story, *Betrayed*, has been translated into more than twenty languages.[31]

He found, as have Lapides and others, that Jesus' words in the gospel of Luke have proved true: "Everything must be fulfilled that is written about me in the Law of Moses, the Prophets and the Psalms."[32] It was fulfilled, and only in Jesus—the sole individual in history who has matched the prophetic fingerprint of God's Anointed One.

CONCLUSION:
THE VERDICT OF HISTORY

As I was getting ready to complete my investigation of the child in the manger, I kept returning to the fact that Christmas doesn't mean very much without Easter.

That's because Christians believe that Jesus wasn't born into this world merely to identify with us, console us, or even lead us. His assignment from the outset, they claim, was to die for us—to actually lay down his life as a spiritual payment for the wrongdoing we've done, so that we can be released from the penalty we owe. It's his-life-for-ours, with the result being, as the old Christmas carol "Hark! The Herald Angels" says, "God and sinners, reconciled."

So while the eyewitness evidence gave me confidence in the reliability of the Gospels, the scientific evidence corroborated their trustworthiness, the profile evidence showed that Jesus fulfilled the attributes of God, and the fingerprint evidence established that he's the Messiah, it was the evidence of Easter that really clinched the case for me.

In other words, anyone can claim to be the Son of God, as the baby Jesus grew up to do, but it was his miraculous return from the dead that authenticated that claim once and for all. To me, the evidence was conclusive:

THE EMPTY TOMB

Christ's empty grave is reported or implied in extremely early sources—Mark's gospel and the 1 Corinthians 15 creed that Blomberg mentioned—which date so close to the event that they could not possibly have been products of legend, Dr. William Lane Craig told me.

Also, the site of Jesus' tomb was known to both Christian and Jew alike, so it could have been checked out by doubters. In fact, nobody—not even the Roman authorities or Jewish leaders—ever claimed that the tomb still contained Jesus' body. Instead they were forced to invent the absurd story that the disciples, despite lacking motive or opportunity, stole the body—a theory not even the most skeptical critic believes today.

THE EYEWITNESSES

The evidence for the post-resurrection appearances of Jesus didn't develop gradually over the years as mythology distorted memories of his life. Rather, as Dr. Gary Habermas said, the resurrection was "the central proclamation of the early church from the very beginning."

The ancient creed in 1 Corinthians 15 mentions specific individuals who encountered the risen Christ, and Paul even urged first-century doubters to personally talk with these eyewitnesses to determine the truth of the matter for themselves. In fact, Paul's own conversion from skepticism to faith, like that of James', is inexplicable apart from the resurrection.

In addition, the book of Acts is littered with extremely early affirmations of Jesus' resurrection, while the Gospels describe numerous encounters in detail. In all, more than 515 individuals met the risen Christ in a variety of circumstances over several weeks. "The appearances of Jesus are as well-authenticated as anything in antiquity," said

British theologian Michael Green. "There can be no rational doubt that they occurred."

THE CLINCHER

Dr. J. P. Moreland pointed out that the disciples were in a unique position to know whether the resurrection actually happened, and they were willing to go to their deaths proclaiming it was true.

Moreland's logic was persuasive. "Obviously," he said, "people will die for their religious convictions if they sincerely believe they are true." Religious fanatics have done that throughout history. While they may strongly believe in the tenets of their religion, however, they don't know for a fact whether their faith is based on the truth. They're simply not in a position where they can know for sure. They can only believe.

In stark contrast, the disciples were in the unique position to know for a fact whether Jesus had returned from the dead. They said they saw him, touched him, and ate with him. And knowing the truth of what they actually experienced, they were willing to die for him.

Had they known this was a lie, they would never have been willing to sacrifice their lives. Nobody willingly dies for something that they know is false. They proclaimed the resurrection to their deaths for one reason alone: they *knew* it was true, because they had personally encountered and experienced the risen Jesus.[33]

So, ironically, it's the evidence for Easter that provided the decisive confirmation for me that the Christmas story is true: that the freshly born baby in the manger was the unique Son of God, sent on a mission to be the savior of the world.

GOD'S GREATEST GIFT

After spending nearly two years investigating the identity of the Christmas child, I was ready to reach a verdict. For me, the evidence was clear and compelling. Yes, Christmas is a holiday overlaid with all sorts of fanciful beliefs, from flying reindeer to Santa Claus sliding down chimneys. But I became convinced that if you drill down to its core, Christmas is based on a historical reality—the incarnation: God becoming man, Spirit taking on flesh, the infinite entering the finite, the eternal becoming time-bound. It's a mystery backed up by facts that I now believed were simply too strong to ignore.

I had come to the point where I was ready for the Christmas gift that Perfecta Delgado had told me about years earlier: the Christ child, whose love and grace are offered freely to everyone who receives him in repentance and faith. Even someone like me.

So I talked with God in a heartfelt and unedited prayer, admitting and turning from my wrongdoing, and receiving his offer of forgiveness and eternal life through Jesus. I told him that with his help I wanted to follow him and his ways from here on out.

There was no choir of heavenly angels, no lightning bolts, no tingly sensations, no audible reply. I know that some people feel a rush of emotion at such a moment; as for me, there was something else that was equally exhilarating: there was the rush of reason.

Over time, however, there has been so much more. As I have endeavored to follow Jesus' teachings and open myself to his transforming power, my priorities, my values, my character, my worldview, my attitudes, and my relationships have been changing—for the better. It has been a humbling affirmation of the apostle Paul's words: "Therefore, if anyone is in Christ, he is a new creation; the old has gone, the new has come."[34]

And now, what about you?

Perhaps, like the first-century sheepherders, your next step should be to further investigate the evidence for yourself. You need to get answers to the spiritual sticking points that are keeping you from following Jesus. It's my hope that you'll promise yourself at the outset that when the facts are in, you'll reach your own verdict in the case for Christmas.

Or maybe you're more like the magi. Through a series of circumstances, including the reading of this book, you've maneuvered your way through the hoopla and glitter and distractions of the holiday season, and now you've finally come into the presence of the baby who was born to change your life and rewrite your eternal destination.

Go ahead, talk to him. Offer your worship and your life. And let him give you what Perfecta Delgado called the greatest gift of all.

Himself.

FOR FURTHER EVIDENCE

Blomberg, Craig. *The Historical Reliability of the Gospels.* Downers Grove, Ill.: InterVarsity, 1987.

Brown, Michael L. *Answering Jewish Objections to Jesus: Messianic Prophecy Objections.* Grand Rapids, Mich.: Baker, 2003.

Bruce, F. F. *The New Testament Documents: Are They Reliable?* Grand Rapids, Mich.: Eerdmans, 2003.

Craig, William Lane. *Reasonable Faith.* Westchester, Ill.: Crossway, 1994.

Copan, Paul, ed. *Will the Real Jesus Please Stand Up? A Debate Between William Lane Craig and John Dominic Crossan.* Grand Rapids, Mich.: Baker, 1998.

Habermas, Gary. *The Historical Jesus.* Joplin, Mo.: College Press, 1996.

Strobel, Lee. *The Case for Christ.* Grand Rapids, Mich.: Zondervan, 1998. Also available in student edition.

Strobel, Lee. *The Case for Faith.* Grand Rapids, Mich.: Zondervan, 2000. Also available in student edition.

Wilkins, Michael J., and J. P. Moreland, eds. *Jesus Under Fire.* Grand Rapids, Mich.: Zondervan, 1995.

NOTES

1. See Luke 2:8–18, *The Message*.
2. Lee Strobel, "Youth's Testimony Convicts Killers, but Death Stays Near," *Chicago Tribune* (October 25, 1976).
3. Irenaeus, *Adversus haereses* 3.3.4.
4. Karen Armstrong, *A History of God* (New York: Ballantine/Epiphany, 1993), 82.
5. William Lane Craig, *The Son Rises: Historical Evidence for the Resurrection of Jesus* (Chicago: Moody Press, 1981), 140.
6. Armstrong, *A History of God*, 79.
7. First Corinthians 15:3–7.
8. For the full story, see Joe McGinniss, *Fatal Vision* (New York: New American Library, 1989). For a description of the evidence, see: Colin Evans, *The Casebook of Forensic Detection* (New York: John Wiley, 1996), 277–80.
9. See Luke 1:1–4.
10. Norman Geisler and Thomas Howe, *When Critics Ask* (Wheaton, Ill.: Victor, 1992), 385.
11. John Ankerberg and John Weldon, *Ready with an Answer* (Eugene, Ore.: Harvest House, 1997), 272.
12. Acts 1:3.
13. John 1:14a.
14. John McRay, *Archaeology and the New Testament* (Grand Rapids, Mich.: Baker, 1991), 155, emphasis added.
15. Frank Zindler, "Where Jesus Never Walked," *American Atheist* (Winter 1996–97), 34.
16. Jack Finegan, *The Archaeology of the New Testament* (Princeton: Princeton Univ. Press, 1992), 46.
17. Ian Wilson, *Jesus: The Evidence* (1984; reprint, San Francisco: HaperSanFrancisco, 1988), 67.
18. John 1:46.
19. See Matthew 2:13–23.
20. Clifford Wilson, *Rocks, Relics and Biblical Reliability* (Grand Rapids, Mich.: Zondervan; Richardson, Tex.: Probe, 1977), 120, cited in Ankerberg and Weldon, *Ready with an Answer*, 272.

21. Gary Habermas, *The Verdict of History* (Nashville: Nelson, 1988), 169.

22. Marla Donato, "That Guilty Look," *Chicago Tribune* (April 1, 1994).

23. Josh McDowell and Bart Larson, *Jesus: A Biblical Defense of His Deity* (San Bernardino, Calif.: Here's Life, 1983), 62–64.

24. Evans, *Casebook of Forensic Detection*, 98–100.

25. Isaiah 53:3–9, 12.

26. For basic details on fulfilled prophecies, see Josh McDowell, *Evidence That Demands a Verdict* (1972; reprint, San Bernardino, Calif.: Here's Life, 1986), 141–77.

27. Peter W. Stoner, *Science Speaks* (Chicago: Moody, 1969), 109.

28. Acts 3:18, NASB.

29. For a discussion of the Daniel prophecy, see Robert C. Newman, "Fulfilled Prophecy as Miracle," in R. Douglas Geivett and Gary R. Habermas, eds., *In Defense of Miracles* (Downers Grove, Ill.: InterVarsity, 1997), 214–25.

30. For example, see Michael L. Brown's trilogy: *Answering Jewish Objections to Jesus: General and Historical Objections*; *Answering Jewish Objections to Jesus: Messianic Prophecy Objections*; and *Answering Jewish Objections to Jesus: Theological Objections*, all published by Baker Books of Grand Rapids.

31. Stan Telchin, *Betrayed!* (Grand Rapids: Chosen, 1982).

32. Luke 24:44.

33. For more details on my interviews with Craig, Habermas, and Moreland, see Lee Strobel, *The Case for Easter* (Grand Rapids: Zondervan, 2003).

34. Second Corinthians 5:17.